This book may be kept

HUMAN ADVENTURES

IN

HAPPY LIVING

HUMAN ADVENTURES
IN
HAPPY LIVING

by

William L. Stidger

NEW YORK

Fleming H. Revell Company

LONDON AND GLASGOW

New York: 158 Fifth Avenue
London, E. C. 4: 29 Ludgate Hill
Glasgow, C. 2: 229 Bothwell Street

TO

ACKNOWLEDGMENT

THE AUTHOR AND the publishers appreciate the co-operation of the following other authors and publishers for their generous permission to reprint copyrighted material in this book:

War Cry, Christian Advocate, and *Christian Herald,* for material already published in those magazines.

Guideposts, for permission to reprint "The Soul Can Split the Skies in Two."

Houghton-Mifflin Company, for permission to quote from the poem "Abraham Lincoln," by John Drinkwater.

The Macmillan Company, for permission to use "Foreign Missions In Battle Array," from Vachel Lindsay: *General Booth Enters Heaven and Other Poems,* copyright 1913 by the Macmillan Company and used with their permission. From *The Everlasting Mercy* and *The Widow of The Bye Street,* copyright 1916, by John Masefield, used by permission of the Macmillan Company, publishers.

"The White Haired Man," from *The Lion and The Rose,* copyright 1948, by May Sarton. Reprinted by permission of the author and the publisher, Rinehart and Company, Inc., New York.

"Education," taken from *Death and General Putnam And 101 Other Poems,* by Arthur Guiterman, published and copyrighted by E. P. Dutton and Company, Inc., New York.

Mr. Berton Braley, for permission to quote "The Battle Might Be Gory," etc.

Mr. Virgil Markham, for permission to quote from various poems written by his distinguished poet-father, Edwin Markham.

CONTENTS

I

LIVING IN THE CLEAR . . .

WE STOPPED IN front of a dilapidated farmhouse in a town near Statesville, North Carolina, one fine June morning. A strange scene greeted us. Leading from the main highway to the farmhouse were the stumps of what once had been beautiful pine trees, which must have formed a tunnel of shade on a hot day. The two rows of freshly sawed-off stumps told a dramatic tale of sacrifice and stewardship.

A bright red cardinal flashed across our path as we alighted from our automobile; the fragrant scent of wistaria and honeysuckle was wafted lightly on the fresh morning air. A mocking bird was singing its little heart out, as glad as we were to be alive that wonderful day. Especially happy we were as we ended our visit at the simple farmhouse, happy because we had met an unforgettable character; because our hearts were lifted to higher levels through the glorious adventure in Christian living we had heard.

Dr. Charles Bowles, a young Methodist pastor had told me about the possibilities of the visit the day before, when he remarked, "You seem to be interested in laymen who tithe and have a deep sense of Christian service. We have a farmer about six miles out of town named Harvey Wood Murdock, who not only tithes, but gives everything he has; and he has a lot of it, because he owns oil and gas wells in Oklahoma."

"He sounds interesting; may I have a visit with him?"

"Yes, you may, and I shall arrange it. You are in for the surprise of your life for the man and his wife live as you might call it—primitively."

"What do you mean by 'primitively,' Charles?"

"I mean that he has an immense annual income from oil and gas, and yet he has no modern improvements in his home. Lives by oil light, has no electricity, no telephone, no gas or oil heat; uses an old-fashioned wood burning stove, no indoor toilet. He lives primitively when he might have all the modern comforts of life if he didn't have such a simple, almost naïve sense of Stewardship in handling his large income."

"That kind of a man intrigues me, Charles. Take me to him."

The next morning, around six o'clock, we started out to see Mr. Murdock. To see a North Carolina farmer you must arise early!

Thirty minutes later we drove down a flower-bordered side road into a group of dilapidated farm buildings. The fresh morning air was scented with wistaria, honeysuckle and magnolias. And the singing of the bird chorus of orioles, tanagers, cardinals, and mocking birds in the trees was accompanied by the humming of bees and the crowing of roosters.

There was an old hay-strewn barn and an old-fashioned well, such a well as must have inspired the writing of *The Old Oaken Bucket*. An elderly, grey-mustached farmer, well-tanned, with shoulders bent, was drawing water from the well when we arrived. Above the well was a canopy of wistaria in full bloom and in a tangled thatch sat a mother cardinal on her nest—a scene to make the heart jump from sheer breath-taking ecstasy.

The old farmer shook hands with us gravely. Our visit was an event to him, and a slow, pleased smile appeared on his wrinkled, weather-beaten face. It was an event to us also, as it turned out. He gave us a drink of cool water from an old hollowed-out gourd. We sat down on the curb of the well and talked for a few minutes before going inside the farmhouse to meet his wife.

As I sat there I put my first question to him. It was about the double row of freshly cut pine stumps which bordered the path to his house and which looked as if they had been sawed down within the week: "Why did you cut down those beautiful trees and lose their shade and beauty for your home?"

Harvey Murdock answered my very blunt question as simply as a little child: "I cut them down to build a little church over yonder across the fields," pointing to the east. And then he added, "Lumber is scarce this year in these parts, and the church needed them. Wife and I talked it over and decided that, 'while only God can make a tree,' as that Yankee poet said, it's up to man to put trees to some good use. God certainly made trees for some good purpose besides shelter and to add beauty to a farmhouse, so we cut 'em down and gave them to build a Community church. Doesn't that make good sense, Doctor?"

"It certainly does, Mr. Murdock," I responded. Later he took me over to see the pine lumber lying in front of a newly-constructed foundation for a church.

"Those stumps don't look as nice in my yard as the trees did, but they'll look mighty nice when they are the altar,

roof, and walls of a church in which to worship the
Heavenly Father. My father planted them and they have
sheltered me all my life. Now I am getting old, and it
gives me a fine feeling to know that they are to shelter
thousands of little children and adults within the walls of
a church."

"It's a funny thing about this giving business; the more
you give, the more you get; only the things you get in return are spiritual things, things which satisfy the soul."

"Take us, now. Several months ago my wife and I decided to give ten thousand dollars to a school, and I wrote
out a check then and there and forgot all about it. That
very morning a cardinal bird started to build her nest in
our wistaria vines above the well out there—where I gave
you the drink of water. We watched the bird build her
nest, lay her eggs, hatch them, and then we watched the
young ones learn to fly; and that's about all anybody ought
to ask from life in one summer. That's more satisfying
than money to us, isn't it, mother?" turning to his quiet
wife. "Isn't it, Doctor?" turning to me.

He had asked me a question. Such a question I had not
been asked in all my years of interviewing unusual characters among the great and the near-great.

I was dumfounded. It didn't seem possible that anyone
could talk as he did—in this mechanised, sophisticated age
—and not be putting on an act. Yet he was as simple,
naïve and gentle as a child when I searched his expression,
neither boasting nor trying for an effect. He was in earnest; he meant it. He was stating a fact of life as he saw it,
setting forth his philosophy of Christian living, and it was
as serious a matter with him as the cutting down of the
beautiful pine trees had been. It was only what a Chris-

tian should do, and here was just what he should expect as a reward: that nest of cardinals in his wistaria vines. But, to resume, he had asked me a question, and it was up to me to answer it.

"You are right, Mr. Murdock, and though I had never thought of it in just that way, you're *right!* God does reward us in His own way when we serve Him and give all that we have for and to Him. My friend Edwin Markham, the poet, used to say to his son Virgil when the boy was five years old, that he could write a poem about anything— absolutely anything, and that everything in life was poetry —and religion, if you had the eye and the heart to see.

"One morning Virgil came running to his father, dragged him by the hand to the window, pointed to a bird's nest in a bush just outside the window, and said, 'You say that you can write a poem about anything, father. Write one about that bird's nest.'

"And this is the poem that Edwin Markham, the poet-father wrote:

'There are three green eggs
  In a small, round pocket;
And the wind will blow
  And the gales will rock it;
Till three little birds
  On the thin edge teeter;
And our God be glad,
  And the world be sweeter.' "

Mr. Murdock's eyes expressed his understanding and his delight as I quoted the poem.

"That's it! 'And our God be glad and the world be sweeter.' I like that line! That's what I always wanted to say myself. God is glad when a bird is born, so glad that

He wants us to share His happiness. He gives us birds and flowers and trees as a reward for something we do which He likes. That's reasonable. That's why He sent us that cardinal bird to nest in the wistarias. That's what I mean, Doctor. 'And our God be glad and our world be sweeter!' I've waited all my life to hear that said."

The farmer went on, "Now, take last week. We gave an orphanage a few thousand dollars, and this morning you came to visit us, and that's something! It always works out that way. You give something and you get something more in return than you gave. The Bible says, 'Cast your bread upon the waters, and it will return,' and, as I always add, 'with butter and jam on it.' " He laughed at his adaptation of the Biblical verse, but we all understood what he meant and we laughed with him, a warm, tender, and kindly laugh.

Then, as an afterthought, he added, "Besides, as some Chinese sage once said, Doctor, 'To whom much is given, from him much is expected.' God gave us those oil and gas wells out in Oklahoma and He expects us to give it back in some practical ways. Doesn't it make sense, Doctor?"

All through our interview, this wise philosopher was continually asking questions like that, and although I had come to ask him questions, he had asked me as many as I had asked him.

I agreed with him.

Presently we entered the simple, unadorned, plainly furnished farmhouse. Tidy and immaculately clean, it certainly was bare of what most of us would term the modern essentials of living in these days of electric ranges, refrigerators, steam heat, and running water.

We sat and talked for two hours, talked of his conversion at the altar of the church when he was a mere boy in his teens. He remarked, very simply, "God came to me and changed my life forever." We talked of his long service in the little country church, of how he loved to sing in the choir, of how he met his wife in the same church. "At a singin' bee." He said he was one of a family of six boys, and had wanted to "go West." "I want to go West, Pa! Like the other boys!"

"Harvey, you'll go West like the other boys, but you're a home boy, and you'll get lonesome. You'll come right back to this old farm as sure as shootin', son," said his father.

"No, I won't, Pa!"

But after two years that old father said to him as they sat together on the curb of the old wistaria-covered well one twilight night, "Now, Harvey, son, you can go West like the other boys."

Harvey made money in the West, in fact, made a small fortune the first seven years and then lost it all. He became seriously ill and had to be carried on a stretcher from Wyoming, where he owned a sheep ranch, to Texas, and then to Warm Springs, where he hoped the waters would cure the rheumatism that had shattered his health. Praying desperately to the God whom he had always followed, he took the warm spring baths, had faith, and, sure enough, he got well after a whole year lying flat on his back.

"It was a miracle from God. I got well! It was an answer to prayer and I made a vow that if I got well I would do more than tithe my income as I had always done. My vow was that I would give ALL to Him. God has always stood by me and I shall always stand by Him."

All this was said as simply as if he were announcing the state of the weather. Then he continued:

"Back in 1905 I filed on 160 acres of land in 'No-Man's Land.' That's what we called that strip of land between Oklahoma and Texas, because it looked like a desert and was the most forsaken spot in this country."

"But it turned out not to be so forsaken as we thought. I raised corn and made a small fortune doing it. Then God gave us oil and gas on that 'No-Man's Land.' He always stands by you when you stand by Him. I never knew it to fail. First, He got me converted, then sent me West. He cured me of rheumatism at His Warm Springs. He gave me land between Oklahoma and Texas and gave me oil and gas. So, you see, it's *His* money, after all!"

"Doctor, I was raised right. My parents brought me up in the church. I've always given to the church because I was taught that way. I never knew any other way. After meeting my obligations I've always given what was left over to the church. You see, I didn't feel that it belonged to me, for it was given to me and I just held it in trust. I always met my obligations first. I never in my life asked any man to endorse a note for me. I *always lived clear!*"

"What do you mean when you say, 'I always lived clear'?"

He cleared his throat and smiled, put his gnarled old hand on my shoulder in a kindly gesture, like a father, and said, "I mean that I always pay my just debts to everybody first, and then I pay my just debts to God, who gave me everything I have which makes me happy: my wife, my church, my religion, my farm, my gas and oil, my friends, my rich memories of life, my cardinals, magnolia trees, wistarias, and—my pine trees. But some things I have to give back, and the pine trees were the things that I had to give back. That's what I mean when I say, 'I always live clear!'" He went on: "I had my ups and downs in Oklahoma, raisin' corn before I struck oil and gas. That was five years ago, and, as I stood on my back porch, bareheaded, and the prairie winds blowin', that well looked like a railroad engine blowin' off steam more than two hundred feet in the air five miles away. Wife and I felt that we could give to the church in a big way, for I'm never one to leave God out of anything—health, sickness and need, or wealth. I turned to Him in my year of sickness and He stood by me. I said to my wife that morning as we stood on the porch and saw the well shootin' high into the air, "Now that I've licked that old rheumatism and we've got the gas well and a little wealth, we're goin' to give it to God, ain't we, darlin'?" She looked up and said, "Yes, darlin'."

I was so impressed with the old farmer's wealth and the decided contrast between the way he lived and the way he could have lived that I had an irresistible impulse to ask him a question which might be termed decidedly personal and impertinent. I followed my impulse, and asked:

"Mr. Murdock, I've been sitting here listening with great interest to your most unusual story, and looking about me, I have wanted to ask you a very personal question."

"Ask it, son." That 'son' got me, for we were only about ten years apart.

"Mr. Murdock, it seems strange to me that, with all of your wealth, you live so simply. You have no electric range, and TVA power so near; no hot and cold water, in fact, no running water at all in this house. No plumbing, heating, or electric facilities."

"Yes, what of it, Doctor?"

"But, man alive, with your income you could have everything—radio, oil heat, electric lights, fireless cooker, and all comfort and luxury. I don't understand it!"

A puzzled look came into his kindly eyes, and then he looked at me and said, "That's a funny thing, Doctor Stidger, but my wife and I were talkin' about that very thing last night, settin' out there on the well curb listenin' to the mockin' birds singin'. And do you know what we decided?"

"No, what did you decide, Mr. Murdock?"

"We decided that, after we get the Children's Home built, and the Home for the Aged built at Charlotte, which will cost fifty thousand dollars, and the ten-thousand-dollar pledge for the North Carolina College Advance paid for, our Community church built, and a few more church things in which we are interested finished, we just might up and git us runnin' water, an indoor closet, furnace, electric lights, and other modern improvements. But we don't dare do it until we get them things done."

Then, as though it were a great joke that they should have the comforts of life, he laughed loudly, and the laugh was contagious.

He paused for some time, with a half-smile on his face. Finally he got up from his chair and walked over to a window. He looked out at his cardinal bird sitting on her nest in the wistaria vines above his deep, cool well, and put the final touch on as fine a philosophy for happy living as I have ever heard by saying, "For fifty years I have walked over to this window each morning after I lighted the wood fire in the stove, to see what kind of a day it was going to be. Now, this particular morning it was bright and sunny. My mocking birds [he always said "my"] and my cardinals were singin' fit to kill, as if their little throats would bust. The wistaria and honeysuckle scent was pourin' through the window on the dew. But on mornings when it is dark and rainy I always say as I look out, 'Thank you, God! This is exactly the kind of a day I wanted!' And it always is!"

II

"O MOTHER, WHEN I THINK OF THEE—"

A POET HAS said:

> "O Mother, when I think of thee,
> 'Tis but a step to Calvary."

I think I know what that poet meant, for I had a mother like that, and one of the first memories I have of her is a certain Christmas down in Moundsville, West Virginia, when she taught me the most vivid lesson in sacrifice that I have ever learned.

My mother came from a banker's home in Winfield, Kansas. My father ran away from his West Virginia home in the early '80s and got a job in a grocery store in Winfield, Kansas. The wealthy banker's daughter, Etta Robinson, used to come to the grocery store to buy food for her home, and fell in love with Roy Stidger, as he did with her, and they were married.

My father took Etta away from that wealthy home, and brought her back to Moundsville, West Virginia. In twelve years she had five children, did all of her own work, gave up luxuries. Her children were born at home, not in a hospital. She died at thirty-two, a gloriously beautiful person, deeply religious, and with laughter in her soul, the memory of which is still vivid to me.

On a Christmas when I was about seven and the oldest of the five children, my mother called me and said that as my father was unemployed there would be no Christmas for us children unless she and I made it. We set to work stringing cranberries and popcorn, making presents ourselves. My mother said to me, "You are the oldest, Willie, and, of course, you won't care about having a meagre homemade Christmas, but the younger children will care."

I *did* care but I put up a strong bluff, and mother and I started in to make a homemade Christmas for five children, simply because we were too poor to have any other kind.

Then one eventful day a letter arrived from Winfield, Kansas, in a long official-looking envelope, with "Bank of Winfield" heavily engraved on its flap. Mother opened it and read it to me, since I was the oldest. This is what it said:

> "Dear Etta:
> I happen to know that you have not had a new coat, dress or hat since you were married. I have secret ways of finding out those facts. I mean that you shall have some new clothes, so I am enclosing my check for $100.00 with the distinct understanding that you are to spend every cent of this money on yourself and not on the children.
> Affectionately,
> W. C. Robinson."

Mother wept, giggled, and laughed as she read me the letter. To my child mind it was a hilarious moment and I said, "Mother, will you let me go with you to buy a hat, coat, and a new dress?"

She looked at me with a puzzled look in her blue eyes, and I swear to you that after fifty years have passed, I can still see her face as if that idea had never occurred to her, and she asked, "To buy *what* dress, Willie?"

"The dress Uncle Will says you must buy with that money, Mother."

She laughed again, a laugh that had humor, delight, and —a sense of victory. I shall never forget it. It still rings in my memory after I have become a man in middle life who has children and grandchildren of his own.

One Sunday, in St. Louis, Missouri, I was preaching about the sacrificial spirit of mothers, and I told that story. Sitting in a pew was Branch Rickey, owner of the Dodgers in Brooklyn, with his wife and small son. At the end of the story I asked a rhetorical question, as many a preacher has done, not expecting an answer. I said, "Does anyone here in this audience think that my mother spent that money on her own Christmas?"

Much to my surprise, and to the great surprise of his father, the young son of Branch Rickey, piped up so that the whole congregation heard him, "No, sirree!"

I was startled, the audience laughed, and the boy, realising what he had done, blushed in confusion and hid his reddening face in his mother's dress. It was embarrassing for the boy, amusing to the audience, but hilarious to me. The boy instinctively knew that no mother would spend an unexpected windfall on herself no matter what the letter demanded, for all children know about the sacrificial spirit of mothers.

Only a few months ago, Betty Oxnam, daughter of Bishop G. Bromley Oxnam, was in my home, and as we sat around the wood fire talking, our conversation fell into the theme of the eagerness of mothers to give up for their children, and Betty told me about something that had happened in their home when she and Phil, her brother, were children.

One day the Oxnam children were talking about the fact that when an extra piece of cake was left over at a meal, or there was just money enough to get dresses for the girls and not enough left over; or when there was some choice tidbit and mother always seemed to want it for someone else besides herself, Phil said to Betty, in a general philosophical comment on the ways of mothers, "Isn't it funny, Betty, Mother never wants anything!"

Phil Oxnam had discovered a great truth, the same truth which I had discovered through this early childhood experience with my mother, that Branch Rickey's son had discovered for himself, namely, that mothers are sacrificial.

> "O Mother, when I think of thee,
> 'Tis but a step to Calvary."

And all of us had discovered something which Victor Hugo discovered long ago and put into a dramatic episode in one of his fine novels, *Ninety-Three,* a novel in which there is no romantic hero or heroine, in which the hero of the book is a mother—perhaps the only novel of its kind ever written by that great master.

It is set in the aftermath of the French Revolution. The wars are over and the country is devastated, the people starving, just as they are now in most of war-devastated China and Europe.

A French captain and a common soldier were walking through a devastated field one morning. Noticing a stirring in a briar patch beside the road, the captain ordered the soldier to see what was in the briar patch. Cautiously the soldier walked over to the side of the road and ran his bayonet into the briars, when out walked a mother and two small children who had been sleeping all night in the patch. All three of them were emaciated and starving. They had been eating bark from the trees, berries, anything they could find to ward off death by starvation.

The captain, noting their starved look, reached into his knapsack, pulled out a long loaf of French bread and handed it to the mother. She immediately, almost frantically, broke it into two pieces, and handed a piece to each child.

The soldier looked up at his captain and said in the laconic, triphammerlike dialogue which Hugo always uses:

"Sir, the woman is not hungry."

"No, son, it is because *she* is a mother!"

John Masefield in *The Everlasting Mercy* sang that spirit and its reward in this way:

> "He who gives a child a treat
> Makes joybells ring in heaven's street;
> They who give a child a home
> Build palaces in Kingdom Come;
> And she who gives a child its birth
> Brings Saviour Christ again to earth."

No, my mother didn't spend a penny of that check on herself that never-to-be-forgotten Christmas. She spent every cent of it on us children and she gave us such a hilarious, joyous Christmas that all of us, now grown to adulthood with families and grandchildren of our own, have never forgotten it. We still call that day, "Mothers' Christmas." And on that unforgettable day she taught us all the real meaning of sacrifice in a way that we shall remember forever.

Yes, there is something Christlike in the spirit of motherhood, and I was so moved by my discovery of that fact that I once wrote a little beatitude:

Blessed are the mothers of the earth for they have combined the practical and the spiritual into one workable way of life.

They have darned little stockings, mended little dresses, washed little limbs and faces, and have pointed little eyes to the stars, and little souls to the eternal things; to Christ and to God the Father of us all.

Blessed are the mothers of the earth.

III

HE LET THE FACE OF GOD
SHINE THROUGH

I FOUND GOD through my father.

As Edna St. Vincent Millay says in a couplet:

"The soul can split the skies in two
And let the face of God shine through."

My father was a perfect illustration of that couplet. Jesus said, "He that hath seen me hath seen the heavenly Father."

The first memory I have of my saintly father was on an unforgettable spring Sunday when he took me by the hand and walked me up to the top of a West Virginia hill. It was a stiff, hard climb, and my legs ached before we got to the top. Toward the end of the climb my father, who was walking out ahead, kept yelling back at me: "Come a little higher, son! Come a little higher!"

Finally, I caught up with him, and we stopped and turned. Miles and miles of dazzling terrain stretched out before our eyes. My father pointed out the winding curve of the beautiful Ohio River, the hills of Ohio beyond the river.

"The higher you climb, the more beautiful it becomes," he said. "The farther up you get, the wider your vision and the more you can see. It's a great and glorious world, son."

Just then a cardinal flashed past us and alighted on a mountain laurel twig. The laurel was a pinkish white and the leaves a deep green. That cardinal bird was such a flash of colour against that green background that I have never forgotten it.

"That's a cardinal bird, son. We call it a red bird, but bird experts call it a cardinal. God made the cardinals, the Baltimore orioles, the red-winged blackbirds, the scarlet tanagers, the eagles, and the wrens. God did a beautiful thing when He made the birds, didn't He?"

And, somehow, on that beautiful morning my father introduced me to God in a simple, convincing fashion, which made Him seem very real to me.

On that same trip my father would stop and say, "Willie, this is a hickory-nut tree . . . here is a chestnut tree . . . that is a beech tree . . . and here is an oak tree. In the Fall those maple trees will turn golden, that sumach tree will turn crimson, and the oak trees change into tawny brown. In that way God makes the world as beautiful in the autumn as in the spring. God decorates the hills with a golden, crimson tapestry in the fall and carpets the meadows and fields with a golden oriental rug. God is a great artist, son!"

On another memorable Sunday afternoon my father and I were sitting on our front porch, when Max Bachenheimer, our town's only Jew, walked by. He smiled as father greeted him. Then my father told me what a fine, generous family man Max was. He told me how hard Max worked and what a good citizen he was, how faithful he was to his duties. That same afternoon one of our town Negroes also passed by. He was a simple, faithful soul, worked hard, took good care of his large family, always attended church, and tithed his small income. All of this my father told me simply and naturally, and I drank it in.

Then my father said, "Max is a good father, son. He loves his family and looks after them as a father should. That is the way God does. He is the Father of the whole human family, and we are all a part of that family. That's why we pray 'Our Father' in the Lord's Prayer." Through that simple explanation I came to look upon men of all colours, creeds, and nations as a part of the human family. It is a simple formula—but it works.

My father had another simple way of teaching us to see God. He conducted family worship each morning. All five of us children knelt down on our knees at the breakfast table and father prayed for each one of us by name, starting with the youngest and going to the oldest.

"God bless, be with, and care for, May, Reed, Anna, Nona, and Willie." Then each of us went out into the day's activities, adventures, and childhood problems with the memory of father taking each of our names to God.

A dramatic, tender and unforgettable experience which illustrates my father's devotion to the religious life of his children is the one I like to think of as "The Night of the Little Stockings." It happened this way:

Since my mother died when she was in her early thirties, my father had always felt a very deep and definite sense of responsibility for our religious development. There was no sacrifice that he would not make to see that the five of us got to Sunday school and church each Sunday. We always sat in the same church pew, and my father always sat there with us. He did not send us; he took us.

As my father kept a little confectionery store, he had to work until around midnight on Saturdays. We children always went to sleep about nine o'clock and never knew when he got home from the store. But one Saturday night I found out, for I was restless. Shortly after midnight I was awakened by something dropping on the floor.

I looked up out of sleepy eyes, and my father, noticing that I was awake, said to me, "Sorry I awakened you, Willie. I dropped my darning egg."

Then he got down on his weary knees (he had worked from six that morning to midnight) and crawled halfway under my bed to retrieve his ivory darning egg. Watching from sleep-filled eyes, I saw him take that round, smooth darning egg, settle himself into the rocking chair, insert the egg in the heel of a little stocking, stretch the wool heel of that stocking and clumsily, laboriously, but fairly accurately, darn the last little hole in it.

Once he looked up and smiled at me. "Since your mother died, your father has to darn stockings, Willie, so you'll have clean ones with no holes for Sunday school." He didn't say it bitterly, but with a tender smile, which I have never forgotten.

I dropped off to sleep again, but some time later I was awakened by the light shining in my eyes. I yawned, stretched my arms, rubbed my eyes, then looked across the room. There sat my father sound asleep, with the darning egg dangling from his hand, his head slumped on his chest, but his task was completed. Five pairs of little stockings lay in a neat row on the dresser.

I climbed out of bed, walked over to him, and shook him gently by the shoulder. "Father, you'd better get into bed to sleep."

He opened his eyes, then smiled a rueful smile. "Thank you son. I was pretty tired tonight." He took me in his arms and kissed me. "Back to bed, Willie—and—God keep you!"

"God keep you!" was a favorite phrase of his. He never said "God bless you!" but always "God keep you."

But there was another experience, more intimate, personal and close than all of these. In my youth we had an old-fashioned revival in our Simpson church. I, as an adolescent boy, fell under what was then called "conviction." One evening I accepted the "invitation" to go to the altar. They were singing "Just as I am, without one plea but that Thy blood was shed for me." When they came to the phrase "O Lamb of God, I come! I come!" I was so much in earnest, so eager, that I almost ran down the center aisle of the church, threw myself on the altar, began to weep, pray and reach my soul out to—SOMETHING.

Then that SOMETHING came to me. It was simple, direct, and certain—a great sense of peace, quiet, calm, and assurance that I was at one with God. It was an ecstatic experience and yet a quiet one. I wanted to shout. I wanted to laugh and weep, and tell somebody, I opened my eyes, looked up—and right in front of me, kneeling on the other side of the sacred altar was *my father*. He had seen me hurry down the aisle. He had followed me, to pray with and for me. That was like my father. I found God that day, never to lose Him, and my father was there when I found Him.

My father taught me to see God through nature, through a social conception of the great human family whose father is God, through family prayer, and through a direct and simple religious experience.

"The soul can split the sky in two
And let the face of God shine through."

That was my father's way of leading me to see the face
of God, and it is still a good and a certain and a glorious
way.

IV

"A TENDER CARE THAT
NOTHING BE LOST"

SEVERAL YEARS AGO I wrote a book entitled *There Are Sermons in Stories*, and I dedicated it to Dr. Mark Hopkins of San José, California in this way:

> "To Hazel and Mark Hopkins,
> Who made me see in the 'winter
> of my discontent'
> That "If Winter Comes can
> Spring be Far Behind?"

That dedication is founded on long years of a personal friendship with a doctor whom I wish to use as a symbol for all doctors who have the spirit of Christian service in their hearts, which means most of them. That doctor is Mark Hopkins, son of a minister.

Mark Hopkins' father was a humble pastor in California all his days. He never had a great church or a large salary but he raised a fine family in a common-sense way, with personal character and profound social sense.

Mark grew up in a parsonage and used to ride with his father on his ministerial calls—a good training for his later service in calling on many persons who needed his service, affection, and skill.

Significant to me is that so many fine doctors are sons of ministers. As I look back on a long ministry I remember Dr. Herman Wilson, son of a famous preacher father who, in our first little church in San Francisco, took care of us and never charged a penny for his services. Then came Dr. Hopkins in our second church in San José who did the same thing; then Dr. Hannah in Kansas City, who always looked after our needs with no compensation in cash. In fact, I have often heard Dr. Hannah remark, "I tithe a day of every week and give that day to the Lord. I never charge for my services on that day, and whenever you or any of your family are sick it comes under my tithe of service. I love doing it, so don't take away from me that privilege."

When I came to Boston I had a serious illness. A thorough examination was required which took an entire year, with literally hundreds of X-rays, special service, blood tests. So I was much surprised that I received no bill for this treatment and service. I protested to Dr. Frank Lahey, who smiled and said, "When I think of a profession which spends its life serving other people without charge, as do you in your profession, it gives me joy to serve you in the same spirit that you serve mankind."

The medical service not only included all that I have mentioned for myself, but this great doctor and his clinic also performed an operation for goiter on my mother, who came here from West Virginia, and gave her excellent nursing care. All with not a penny of expense to us.

Wherever I have served across this continent I have discovered doctors in every city and in every denomination who were the sons of ministers and who evidently have caught the spirit of Christian service from their fathers. Dr. Leighton Johnson, one of Boston's specialists in eye, ear, nose and throat ailments, is a truly great man, and the son of a truly great Methodist preacher.

The winter of my first year in San José I preached a dramatic sermon on Ian Maclaren's *Beside the Bonnie Briar Bush,* using the characters in that book, a dominie, a father, and old Dr. McClure as the outline. Those who remember that great, tender book will recall old Dr. Mc-Clure and his "tender care that nothing be lost," and his intuitive understanding of the poor wayward girl who journeyed to London and fell among swine and ate of the husks. Then she returned home and her old Scot father was so hardhearted that he was not going to allow her in his home again. It was Dr. McClure who met her at the railroad station in his old buggy, drove her home through the snow, and when he got there found a light in the window to welcome her home.

When I had finished my sermon, Mark Hopkins came up to me and thanked me for it.

I said, "Mark, I thought of you when I was talking about Dr. McClure. You are like him."

"I don't know whether I'm like him or not, but I *do* know that that's the way I feel, and I do know that I *want* to be like him."

Any preacher who reads this chapter will have in his own memory a Dr. Mark Hopkins, a Dr. McClure, a Dr. Hannah, a Dr. Wilson, or a Dr. Johnson, men of the medical profession who felt that they owed a tithe—and more—of their time, talents and skills to humanity in general, for that seems to be the spirit of the profession everywhere.

Many incidents in one's life are vividly remembered. No man could forget that summer afternoon when a Dr. Mark Hopkins removed his daughter's tonsils in his own office. The operation was performed with skill, and with sympathy for the anxieties of the father and mother. Nor could he forget the time when he returned from the Orient suffering from amebic dysentery, and having lost sixty pounds of weight on the Pacific. He well remembers how that doctor patiently and skilfully took his case, and, over a period of months, treated him and licked the dangerous germ, bringing him back to good health, with absolutely no price on his service.

Nor could any man forget a nervous breakdown which incapacitated him for almost a year, when that same doctor invited him to come to California, gave him, rent free, a restful cottage by the sea; gave him costly injections of hormones and vitamins several times a week during that whole period of time, cared for him like a father, and then laughed when he suggested payment for professional services.

Being a pioneer user of the X-ray, Dr. Hopkins had, like many others, not fully realised its dangers. He suffered a bad burn on the back of his left hand and later underwent a serious operation in San Francisco. He was forced to give up his medical and surgical work. His retirement from active work gave me an opportunity to invite him to Boston for a visit and to recuperate, and what a month of joy that was!

He often said, "Well, my father used to preach on the text, 'Bread cast upon the waters,' as he put it in his homely way, would return after many years, with both butter and jam on it. It has proved true in my case, for this stay with you has not only helped to cure my physical ailment, but also has done something much better than that: it has made a new man of me, mentally. You have cured my mind."

During Mark Hopkins' visit I preached on what I called, "Banting's Miracle," a great book, which described the discovery of insulin by Banting and Best. In the sermon I told of the early days of my ministry, when I dreaded what was then spoken of as "sugar in the blood," the technical name being diabetes. The history of such cases was inevitable—gangrene in the toes, then amputation above the ankles, then, months later, amputation below the knees, after which the thighs, the end coming in coma and death. Each case history was known by every doctor and preacher, from the beginning to the end.

That was true until the discovery of insulin—and the discovery came about in this way:

Young Banting, as a boy in Canada, lived on a farm and had a sweetheart whose name was Janie. He loved her because she could run, jump, ski, and skate, and play games as well as any boy. Then he heard mysterious whispering among the elders about "sugar in the blood" in connection with Janie. Then the term "diabetes," although he didn't even know what the word meant. Weeks later he heard the word "coma," which also was a new, mysterious, and ominous-sounding word to this young man. His boy mind received a frightening shock at his first intimate touch with death.

Years passed and he grew to manhood. For many years he had ideas of becoming a missionary, for he always had had the service motive. Later he decided he would like to be a doctor, with the service motive still in his heart. He finally entered Toronto University. While there he started on the research that came to its glorious climax in the discovery of insulin as a control of "sugar in the blood."

I was a young preacher in Detroit, Michigan, in 1922, when Banting's discovery of insulin was announced to the world. The front pages of the morning's newspapers carried a banner headline across the top of the page as large as the announcement of the discovery of our last planet "Pluto," which came later; or an announcement of war or of peace. Its terrific importance was in the one-word headline:

"INSULIN!"

The next night I took a train for Toronto, with the intention of interviewing Dr. Banting and Best, I arrived early in the morning, and with no previous arrangement, took a cab to Toronto University, where I asked the janitor if I could see the doctors.

"Do you have an engagement?" he asked.

I replied, "No, I do not have an engagement, but I'm a minister and I think they'll want to see me."

With a slight hesitation and a doubtful look in his eyes, he ventured, "They're both over there under that stairway. That's their laboratory. They've been there all night, and I doubt if they'll be very excited about seein' you."

They were *not* very excited about seeing me, but they were courteous while I explained that I was a preacher and wanted to talk with them. They smiled wearily and invited me in.

They had a small 4 by 10-foot laboratory under the stairway, and had very limited funds to continue research on insulin. Both were married. Neither one was earning much money—about $2,000 a year. The university was not very seriously concerned about their work, but the men stuck to it through seven long years. Then it clicked, suddenly, and, like a clap of thunder, the experiments were successful. They could control "sugar in the blood," and it is doubtful that there was ever a more beneficent consummation of long years of research in the history of medicine. The discovery meant that even little children suffering with diabetes could live a normal, natural, and complete life with the use of insulin, as has been proved ever since its discovery.

It was years before I knew the story behind this research work. It goes back to the little girl, Janie, Dr. Banting's boyhood sweetheart, and her death that resulted from "sugar in the blood."

In a great book written by Dr. Searle Harris, entitled *Banting's Miracle,* I finally discovered Dr. Banting's motive for his important research. Because he could not forget through the years, winter or summer, night or day, what had happened to his little friend Janie, he gave his talent, time, and practically his life to discovering a control of "sugar in the blood" so that other little Janies should not die at a tender age from that insidious affliction. Back of the research which ultimately brought us insulin was the love motive and the desire to serve humanity—the spirit of "a tender care that nothing be lost."

Said Dr. Mark Hopkins, after listening to my sermon, "That's the way I have watched doctors, research workers, country practitioners live all of my life. That is the universal spirit of my profession. You will notice that the men who have discovered the great miracles of science, insulin, penicillin, streptomycin, seldom make any money out of it themselves. The pharmaceutical houses, the laboratories which manufacture it, yes, they make the money, but never the researchers and discoverers. Service is the tradition of the doctors, surgeons, and research workers and I am proud to be in the tradition, and I hope I have been worthy of that lineage."

This spirit of service and sacrifice has been expressed in literature many times since the days of old Dr. McClure in *Beside the Bonnie Briar Bush*. Sinclair Lewis set it forth magnificently in *Arrowsmith*, in which he expressed his reverence for old Dr. Gottlief in a single line, "I'd black his boots for him." The whole world reveres the man who gives himself in the spirit of Christ always and everywhere, with a reverence that comes close to worship.

Perhaps Dr. Charles Whitehead, the great Harvard philosopher, expressed it for all of us when he gave a new definition of the spirit of God:

"The best symbol under which we can conceive of the nature of God is that of a tender care that nothing be lost."

That expresses the spirit of Dr. Mark Hopkins through forty years of medical practice and surgical service in an American city, and Dr. Mark is a symbol of all medical men all over the world. There is a traditional spirit of Christian service in that great profession which is closely akin to that of the ministry.

V

"A MINISTERING ANGEL THOU!"

Sir Walter Scott has a poem about women which is much more reverent than Kipling's line in *The Ladies*, "I learned about women from her," and which is also more honestly interpretive of the heart of a Christian woman, something which Kipling never seemed to see in his poem.

> "O woman! in our hours of ease,
> Uncertain, coy, and hard to please,
> And variable as the shade
> By the light quivering aspen made;
> When pain and anguish wring the brow,
> A ministering angel thou!"

It is of such a woman that I speak in this chapter, and through the life and spirit of Sadie Hagen I want to symbolise all nurses, for, in a very true sense, her spirit is the essence of all true nurses, the flowering of service, and sacrifice.

I first discovered Sadie Hagen in the New England Deaconess Hospital when my daughter Betty was there for a major operation. One of the first things that Betty said to me about Miss Hagen was, "It is good medicine just to have Miss Hagen come into my room and smile."

Then Betty told me a story about Miss Hagen that she had heard from a young nurse in the hospital. It seems that one day an elderly woman was just recovering from a serious operation and was close to death and knew it.

Miss Hagen, who was then Superintendent of Nurses, walked quietly into her room to see how she was getting along and stood by her bed, lifting a quiet prayer for her, thinking that the woman was asleep. The woman looked up, sensing that Miss Hagen was praying for her. Miss Hagen asked, "What do you want, dear?" ("Dear" was always one of her favorite words.)

"All I need and want, Miss Hagen, is the touch of your hand on my forehead."

The woman's remark sums up the indefinite, mystical, spiritual something which Sadie Hagen has been contributing to thousands of patients at the New England Deaconess Hospital for more than thirty years, during which time she has seen that great hospital grow out of the oil-lamp day to its now modern, well-equipped, scientific service to New England. "All I need is the touch of your hand on my forehead, Miss Hagen." I like to call that type of service "the overtone" of medical service. Throughout her eventful life Miss Hagen has been the symbol of that type of service in all the hospitals of the world and when I tell her story it will be a symbolic tribute and interpretation of literally thousands of nurses who have cared for patients in hospitals all over the world.

"A ministering angel thou," Sir Walter Scott, one of her favorite authors, could have said to "Sister Sadie," as patients have called her for a quarter of a century. How did this woman come to be this "ministering angel"? That is the purpose of this chapter.

Sister Sadie was born in Belfast, Ireland, and that gave her an unfailing sense of humour and fun, which has been one of her dominant characteristics all her life, a most useful characteristic for a nurse in a hospital to have. Her father dealt in fine Irish linens. Hagen and Pratt was the name of her father's company and since most of his trade was in this country he brought his family here when Sadie was ten years old. However, soon after their arrival tragedy struck—the father died. Her mother, a sister and a brother moved from New York City to Newton Upper Falls, near Boston.

As Sadie herself tells it, "In the Newton Upper Falls Methodist Church I came in contact with a wonderful woman named Fisk, and I caught a vision of service to humanity and entered the Deaconess Training School for Nurses, graduating in 1904.

"My first task was to be sent out with all the graduates of that year, not to do nursing but to get the church a hospital. We lived on our eight dollars a month and even in that day it was some job. I remember that a cake of soap cost eight cents, and my roommate and I contributed four cents each and bought it. We had all things in common, halved our expenses and lived somewhat like the early Christians, sharing each with each."

"It must have been a pretty tough life!" I remarked.

"Not a bit of it! Or, if it was, we didn't know it. As I look back on it, I do not remember any happier or more satisfying days in all my life than those days when I was living on eight dollars a month."

"How do you account for that?"

"Because [and tears filled her eyes] we were going to get a hospital and that sustained us. That fact gave us hope, courage, and faith. And we were just simple enough to believe that it could be done. What is more, because of our faith it *was done,* by golly!"

Perhaps that "by golly" is one of the things that makes

everybody love this Irish girl, Sadie Hagen. She knows how to use the vernacular in slang phrases—and under certain provocations (of which she had had many) even stronger vernacular phrases.

She told me what Bishop Daniel Goodsell had said to her graduating class: "All that the Church has to offer you girls is hard work."

"And the first of that hard work had none of the romance of nursing in a nice clean hospital in a nice linen uniform. Not on your life! It consisted in sending all of us out to solicit money all over New England for a new fifty-bed hospital unit. One experience that I had will live in my memory forever and a day.

"One little, humble, poor woman in Vermont gave me fifty cents. She had saved it by agreeing with her family that the whole family would go without butter for two weeks. That touched my heart. Another mill worker's wife gave me two dollars and fifty cents. That was the start of our Hospital Library, which now has several thousand volumes in it."

Finally, with the help of the newly graduated nurses, Sister Sadie actually got the church its hospital, and that was the beginning of one of the best-equipped hospitals in this whole nation. It now has such a great surgeon as Dr. Frank Lahey on its staff and possesses one of the finest cancer and diabetes divisions in this country, in either secular or church hospitals, with Dr. Warren Cook as its efficient superintendent—and Sadie Hagen standing by, in spite of her retirement, as an efficient helper and friendly advisor in a big new advance campaign for money and a new unit.

From 1910 to 1913 Sadie Hagen was not only a "minis-

tering angel," but she was also the efficient superintendent
of the Deaconess Home. In 1912 she opened a now famous
Home for Aged Women in Concord, Mass. I have visited
that home many times and greatly respect its management,
atmosphere, and spirit. Sadie Hagen said to me about its
origin: "I noticed in my hospital work how many aged
women were terror-stricken at the idea of being left de-
pendent and alone in their old age. That inspired me to
start a movement to get a home for such women, and now
it is going successfully and is an established institution in
New England."

In 1920 Sadie became superintendent of Palmer Memorial, a hospital for cancer patients, and in 1930 she
became assistant superintendent of the entire Deaconess-
Palmer organization.

Dr. Shields Warren says of her: "In the days when the
first Palmer Memorial was built, there was no other hospital for advanced cancer sufferers in New England. As a
result of Sadie Hagen's skill in caring for patients at the
old Palmer Memorial, not only did the new Palmer become possible, but a major step was accomplished in pointing the way toward establishment of the state cancer
program and its hospitals."

Yes, of this modern Florence Nightingale it might be
said in the words of Sir Walter Scott:

"When pain and anguish wring the brow,
    A ministering angel thou!"

And I happen to know, personally, that this is true, for
my daughter Betty experienced some of that ministering
angel's spirit. The morning after her operation I was in
her room, frantic with fear. She had not recovered from

the anesthesia. They had stuffed funny little rubber tubes into her nostrils so that she could breathe easier. I had never seen them before. I imagined that their presence was a danger sign. Her lips were cracked and bruised.

I got the idea that the nurses who came and went were too calm, cool, and collected; that my daughter was in danger and nobody cared much. I was tense with anxiety. Then, suddenly, Sadie Hagen came into the room, deftly removed the rubber things from her nostrils, stroked her hot forehead gently, whispered into her unconscious mind. Then Betty opened her eyes, looked up at Sadie Hagen, and in bewildered fashion whispered the one word, "Mother!"

Her mother was not there, but she thought it was her mother. It was just Miss Hagen, but Sadie Hagen *was* her mother at that moment, in a very real sense. As I sat there the next half hour watching that skilled, clever woman, with years of training back of her, with gentle, deft hands and fingers, tenderly bring that girl child of mind back to consciousness, I remembered the elderly woman who said, "All I need is the touch of your hand on my head."

This is what makes me say that through great, tender, kindly, loving Christian service in everyday life, the spirit of Christ truly marches on in the great church hospitals, sanitariums, and rest homes of this nation which have been established by various denominations.

VI

"MISS MARY OF MOUNDSVILLE"

It may be that there is some person in the Church, who, through personal influence, has sent more young persons into definite Christian work than has Miss Mary Scott of Moundsville, West Virginia, but I do not know who that person is.

"Miss Mary," as Moundsville calls her, is most tender and gentle and skilful in directing youth into channels of service. She has the fine art of helping boys and girls attain a knowledge of Christ and His ways. She knows how to make church members, and, ultimately, ministers, and missionaries. These consecrated talents have resulted in fifty or more full-time Christian workers from Moundsville.

When Miss Mary came to Simpson Church, Moundsville, it already had a reputation for sending out Christian workers. "Father Hughes" had conducted a historic revival service in which a group of young men—Edwin H. Hughes, Matt Hughes, Will Stidger, my uncle, and Leroy Stidger, my father, among them—were converted. So Miss Mary had some preparation for the work she did with a later generation.

In her early teens she was converted and decided to become a Christian worker. She did spend a year in a New York City church. Then her mother went blind and Miss Mary came back to Moundsville to take care of Mrs. Scott.

It was not long before she had associated herself with the young persons of Simpson church, and the disappointment she experienced because she could not go in Christian service was changed into satisfaction that she could influence the lives of others in that direction.

Her method was simple and varied. My own experience is an illustration. My mother died when I was nine years of age. There were five children, ranging in age from me to a nine-months-old baby girl. Miss Mary was in her early twenties when that happened, but she had such a sense of sympathy for us that she immediately took all five of us under her care. She mothered us as only a devoted young woman could.

She used to invite me to her home to eat and then talk to me about going to college. None of my family had ever gone to college. But, under her guidance and counsel, I believed that any young man who expected to amount to anything should go to college.

She talked to me about books. With her help I came to feel that anybody who expected to make his mark had to read and know great books. She gave me books, with the suggestion that I read them and tell her about them. Something of this same interest in reading and learning came to other members of our family, so that three of us went to college.

More important, she got us interested in going to church, and ultimately in giving our lives to Christian service. She gently led us down spiritually and mentally productive paths, without our knowing what she was doing. She was a wise leader.

I remember how she invited us to what she called "the Junior Epworth League." I was so young that I didn't understand what she meant. I thought it was something being held "uptown." Somehow, I got that from "Epworth."

Then there is the memory of her teaching tithing and how to give. I was selling newspapers, and frequently put as much as fifty cents or a dollar in the collection plate.

Furthermore, I recall her urging me to go to an oldfashioned revival service, and inviting me to go to the altar and give my life to Christ, and sending me off to college, not only through her guidance but also through some more practical arrangements for my going.

Through all the years since those exciting days she has helped me to keep my soul alive through books. She has written me regularly, and has kept up a keen interest in all my activities. She sent my sister into deaconess work and my brother into a medical career. And what she did for us she has done for hundreds of families. Here is one of the most thrilling adventures in human service that I have ever known.

In the midst of all this service for the world-wide church, Miss Mary has not forgotten her own Simpson church. She has "served all of the chairs," as she puts it, in the Woman's Foreign Missionary Society. She has carried on a correspondence with more than one hundred missionaries. She has had an active interest in the camp grounds at Bethesda, Ohio, where for years she was a leading inspiration and where the "Scotage" is named for her.

Young persons of five generations have looked to her for leadership and inspiration, and untold numbers all over this earth are in the kingdom of God because of her influence.

There is another person in this moving story. She is

"Miss Norma," who cooked the meals and kept the house so that Miss Mary might carry on her personal work and her church work. It is the finest modern equivalent of a Martha-and-Mary household that I have ever known. They are a great team, a glorious combination for Christian service over half a century. All during these years Miss Mary, as the psychologists would say, has sublimated her early desire for Christian service by carefully and prayerfully, lovingly and efficiently leading young people into definite service to take her place where she could not go and be.

We do much writing and talking about the laymen of the church, but here is a lay woman who, for loyalty and leadership, can match any of them. She is "Miss Mary of Moundsville."

VII

"ONWARD THE LINE ADVANCES!"

THE WHOLE MISSIONARY enterprise, I believe, received an impetus during World War II which, if it is earnestly and efficiently capitalized, will advance the whole missionary program more in the next quarter of a century than it has been advanced in the last one hundred years. Why do I say that?

For these reasons:

First, because literally hundreds of thousands of American boys had intimate, personal contact with American missionaries during the recent war. The only homes they knew which made them feel as if they were in the shelter of their own homes were the missionary homes all over this world—the South Seas, the Philippines, Burma, India, China, Korea, and Africa. For the first time in their lives, and through what they saw, they came to have a profound respect for the personal lives of the missionaries, and for the sacrificial, effective service they were rendering. Thousands of these boys wrote home that they were converted to missions and were already contributing to the cause and would do so after the war was over.

Second, at least ten major books, many of which were put into pictures, were written during the war, each of them inspired by the spirit of sacrifice and service that missionaries of all denominations had given to our American soldiers. Several of those books became best sellers during the war. All of them were, in reality, primarily great missionary documents and propaganda for the whole cause of missions, although they were not written for that purpose. It was my feeling during the war that the Mission Boards did not take advantage of these tremendous propaganda and public relations documents for the future advancement of the whole missionary work and in this chapter I am trying to remedy that defect as best I can. All I know is that these great novels and stories of personal experiences in the war, written by and about missionaries themselves, such as *Burma Surgeon* and *The Story of Dr. Wassell,* were the actual wartime stories of devoted missionaries who had the spirit of Christ in their lives before, during, and after the war. "Onward the Line Advances!" is the spirit of the great documents on missionary work, and onward the line will advance, if we, the Church, take advantage of these testimonies to the integrity of the missionary work, and use them for the future promotion of the whole cause.

Vachel Lindsay and I were sitting before my fireplace in Kansas City a few years ago, talking of many things—of God and man, poetry, music, and art. I was startled to hear him say, "Bill, the trouble with you preachers is that you do not seem to appreciate the importance of missions. You don't get the *poetry* of missions, the daring adventure, and the practical down-to-earth quality of the work those missionaries are doing on the foreign field. You talk too much in terms of statistics, figures, and movements, forgetting the romance of missions."

"Perhaps you're right. But what made you bring that up?"

"Because I have just written a poem on missions."

Then he gave me a private first reading of one of his greatest poems. He called it *Foreign Missions In Battle Array*.

"An endless line of splendor,
These troops with heaven for home,
With creeds they go from Scotland,
With incense go from Rome.
These, in the name of Jesus,
Against the dark gods stand,
They gird the earth with valor,
They heed their King's command.

"Onward the line advances,
Shaking the hills with power,
Slaying the hidden demons,
The lions that devour.
No bloodshed in the wrestling—,
But souls new-born arise—
The nations growing kinder,
The child-hearts growing wise.

"What is the final ending?
The issue can we know?
Will Christ outlive Mohammed?
Will Kali's altars go?
This is our faith tremendous—
Our wild hope, who shall scorn?—
That in the name of Jesus
The world shall be reborn!"

I think I have never been more deeply impressed by any poem or any work of art. The fact that a poet like Vachel Lindsay was inspired to write such a poem also impressed me.

An American soldier who was sent to India was billeted in an American missionary's home. He is Royal Bisbee, and I know him well. When he left that home he handed the missionary twenty-five dollars, with the words: "I never had so much respect for missions in my life as I have now. I've seen you folks in action. I've lived in your home. It's the nearest thing to life at home that I've seen, and I'm making a pledge right now to send you a regular contribution so long as I live. So help me, I will."

Another American boy wrote to a missionary in whose home he had stayed after he landed in Burma. He said:

"From now on I'm laying aside five dollars a month from my pay for missions. I am being sent away tomorrow. I'm going to give you fifty bucks, and that will 'pay me up' for a long time. When I get to another station I'll find me a missionary and start paying him every month. When I get home I'll pay it through the church. I'm converted to this missionary business from now on. I used to be indifferent to missions, although I was raised in a Presbyterian church. In fact, I used to dodge going to church when I knew that there was to be a missionary there—but never again! I'm all for missions now that I have seen you in action."

Yes, our attitude toward missions and missionaries was reborn in the war.

A Methodist layman from the Midwest got a letter from his son telling him that he had been staying with a missionary, but that the censor would not permit him to tell his parents where he was. However, he added, "Yesterday I had dinner with Bishop Springer."

The father immediately wired to the Methodist Mission Board in New York and asked them where Bishop Springer was located at that time. The Board wired back that he was stationed in Africa—and the father knew where his son was located. Later the father said to a friend of mine: "My son said that he had never been treated so wonderfully in all his life as Bishop Springer had treated him, and that he soon discovered that the bishop had more power and influence in that part of Africa than the Government had. He had a new respect for the power of missions in international life, and, so far as he is concerned, they will never have to make any speeches to get him to support missions after what he had actually seen in Africa."

No matter where these boys of ours were sent—to Africa, Iceland, China, Burma, India, or the South Sea Islands—they found that the missionaries had been there for a hundred years or more, making the way easy for them by having already won the respect and affection of the natives through medicine, sanitation, prayers, evangelism, and service.

One native in Singapore said to a friend of mine who decided to remain behind, even though his Methodist bishop had ordered him to evacuate: "You missionaries are all that we have left. The Japs have burned our homes, taken all of our property; our friends are scattered; we never needed you so much as now."

Johnny Maxfelder was a young Jewish friend of mine. He was married to an Irish Catholic girl. He had two small sons. Johnny went into the Navy the day after Pearl Harbor, although he had served in the previous war. Within a few months he was on Guadacanal. His wife showed me a letter which Johnny had written her, and this is what he said:

"I'm a Jew and you're a Catholic, but when I landed on this hot tropical island the only clean, decent place I could find was a missionary's home; they have been wonderful to me. I go there at least once a week for dinner and they have taken me in as though I were their own son. I feel as though I had always been part of their family. This man is a doctor, and the natives come from miles around to his clinic. He takes care of all of them and he never thinks of charging them a cent. That looks funny to me as a Jewish boy, Jane, but, I am beginning to understand it. At first I tried to make Dr. Jones see that they were working him, that he was an easy mark; but I soon saw my mistake and now it is all clear to me. He's a Christian, and he almost persuades me to be one too, the way he lives without thought of himself. I told him last week that he could count on me to send him ten dollars a month out of my pay as long as I'm here, and do you know what he did? He said I'd have to send it through our Board when I got back to the States. He wouldn't even take my money!"

It all reminds me of the experience that my Naval lieutenant nephew had in one of the Solomon Islands early in the war. He was walking along a beach when a sun-burned man dressed like a native called out to him, "Hello, buddy, where you from?"

My nephew thought the man was a native, but he soon learned that he was a Yale graduate and a missionary who had been in the islands for ten years. That night he found himself eating dinner in the missionary's home, and, as he wrote me, "It was a whale of a dinner—just like mother used to cook; it even tasted like home! Boy, I'm for missions! The only spot that looks like home on these islands is the compound of the missionaries. And when you get into one of these compounds in a foreign land it's like catching a sight of the American flag. It brings a lump into your throat and a mist into your eyes. These missionaries are our American outposts and we've never found an island where we haven't discovered them there ahead of us. In fact, they've been here for fifty years."

But there is an even wider sense in which foreign missions were reborn in the heart of the American nation. It is illustrated in a piece that a famous columnist recently wrote—David Lawrence in "Today in Washington." He was talking about Madame Chiang Kai-shek's address in Madison Square Garden in New York City. He took his entire column that day to say to millions of American readers:

"What a strange if not mystic lesson the wife of the Generalissimo is teaching in recompense, perhaps, to the America of more than sixty years ago that gave hospitality and inspiration to her father. And what a wonderful thing it would be if the same inspiration could come now to the statesmen who are again promising to redeem mankind!"

That was not a preacher, a bishop, or even a missionary talking. It was a hard-boiled newspaper man. And the thing that had caused him to talk like a preacher was the fact that he had just unearthed the story of how Madame Chiang's father came to this country sixty years ago, of how a Methodist layman took him into his own home, raised him, educated him, sent him to college, brought him up as a Christian. David Lawrence was talking about how that college graduate finally went back to China to become one of China's richest merchants, and how he backed Dr. Sun Yat Sen and helped him to overthrow the Manchu government and bring the Chinese Republic into existence. He was talking about how that father became the parent of the Soong sisters and Soong brothers who have had such an influence in China. Lawrence had discovered what all America is discovering—that one hundred of the great leaders of China today are products of our mission homes, schools, and colleges, that the inspiration of the New China came out of American missions.

Recently I had the good fortune to talk with a great missionary who had lived in the home of Generalissimo Chiang Kai-shek. Here is an intimate story he told a group of us about the Generalissimo, the Bible, and worship in that home: Every morning, no matter how busy the Generalissimo is, he always takes a half-hour, from five to five-thirty, for Bible-reading and devotion, and he always comes out of the silent meditation periods with a light shining in his face, his kindly eyes twinkling.

One morning Madame Chiang Kai-shek heard him pacing up and down his room, talking out loud, going over and over something which he seemed to be memorizing. She knocked and slipped into his room and found him with a Bible in his hands, walking up and down his room, patiently memorizing one of the Psalms.

She said to him: "What in the world are you doing?"

"I'm memorizing a chapter of the Bible."

"But why do you take time to do that when you always have a Bible to carry with you?"

"I do it because I want these great truths to be *inside* of *me,* to be a part of my memory and mind. There will be many times when I am on trains, in an airplane, in a mountain retreat, and I will not have my Bible with me. I want this Bible inside."

I think I know what Chiang Kai-shek meant when he told his wife that he wanted those Bible quotations to be "inside." He meant what an advertising friend of mine in Boston wrote into a four-line verse when he came home out of a Boston blackout and saw the lights of his own home shining through the lowered blinds:

> "When evening comes and shadows fall,
> And darkness hovers over all;
> When dimmed out, dreary hours begin,
> Thank God, we've still the light within."

That's it, "the light within." Chiang Kai-shek and Madame Chiang Kai-shek—they have that light within—"the great hope who shall scorn, that in the name of Jesus, the world shall be reborn?"

One dramatic illustration of this "light within" testimony came out of the Madison Square Garden address by Madame Chiang Kai-shek which most reporters entirely missed, and that was the note of personal testimony, unabashed and unapologetic, from that great, cultured Chinese woman-statesman. We have heard some of our politicians and statesmen talk *about* religion and *about* God, as if it were expected of them by history and tradition. They always manage to "drag" God in, as I heard one reporter put it. I am not now trying to criticize that recognition of God; I am simply saying that when this frail, porcelain-like woman spoke, her eyes flashing, her voice ringing with sincerity, we all felt that she was giving an old-fashioned testimony to the place that religion and Christ have in her inner life. It sounded a good deal like the testimonies we have all heard in old-time prayer meetings, only this particular prayer meeting took in the whole world by radio short-wave. This woman stood up and testified that Christ had done something for her mother, her father, her husband, herself, her nation—and there was the ring of sincerity in it. It was no official sop to religious people. It was no statesman's gesture of diplomacy.

It was a down-to-earth, simple, unaffected, almost naïve and childlike testimony to the fact that Christ and His way of living, thinking, dying, had done something to the inner lives of two generations of Chinese leaders.

This avalanche of testimony to "The Faith Tremendous" which is at the very heart of our individual missionaries and the whole missionary movement is not confined to American soldiers who saw the results of missions for the first time at first-hand, or to such world leaders as the Chiangs. It got into the movies, through *Keys of the Kingdom, Thirty Seconds Over Tokyo, Letter from New Guinea, Burma Surgeon,* and *The Story of Dr. Wassell* by James Hilton. When a man like Hilton takes time out to write about a man like Wassell—well, that *is* news. Wassell was a missionary doctor from our Midwest serving in China. He was caught by the Japanese invasion in Java and became a hero overnight in his work with wounded American soldiers. Some people marvelled at him—but they wouldn't have marvelled had they known that for years he had been doing exactly the same kind of work for the Chinese.

President Roosevelt mentioned Dr. Wassell in a national broadcast, saying that to the wounded boy the medico was "almost a Christian shepherd, devoted to his flock." That was well put. This lone doctor got twelve wounded boys to safety and the seacoast in Java, displaying a brand of courage the world will envy when it reads this story.

On the little Dutch boat that took this party of Americans to Australia Wassell watched a strange courtship. McGuffey, a ne'er-do-well sailor, became engaged to a little refugee girl. When the doctor jocularly warned her about McGuffey's character, she said: "I was the last woman out of Sumatra. I walked two hundred miles through the jungle and I was nearly killed by wild elephants. But I kept on till I got to the coast, and then I persuaded a native boy to take me in a small boat. The Japanese fired on us and sank the boat, but I managed to swim ashore on Java. Six weeks the whole journey took, and all kinds of people helped me—Dutch, English, native—but, somehow, I didn't meet any Americans till I came aboard this ship. And then—believe me—I felt I could love the worst American sailor in the world. . . . I guess I really don't know what I'm saying. I'm a missionary."

Missionaries are like that—gentle, understanding, forever looking for the best in people, not the worst. They've brought out the best in the worst people in the world; that's their business, and they've made a good job of it. So good that all the rest of us might say with this same Dr. Wassell, as he looks at the little lady, "I take off my hat to the missionaries, and if any young man I knew felt that he had a call that way I'd say, 'On top to you, my lad, you join 'em—they're the salt of the earth.' "

Salt is one word for it. The other is *hope* of the world.

VIII

A CUP OF COLD WATER IN THE JUNGLE

THE GREAT TASK of the church is to awaken this almost primitive sense of a "tender care that nothing be lost," this paternal, maternal sense of human brotherhood, this spirit of "Our Father," with its implication of the human family.

Early in my ministry Dr. Harry Ward presented me with a truly great book by Prince Propotkin. It was entitled *Mutual Aid,* and was written to prove that there was a spirit in the world which was in direct contrast with Darwin's theory of the survival of the fittest. It had chapters proving by documentary evidence that even among savages, barbarians, primitives, and even among birds and animals, there is the spirit of *mutual aid* dominating all life. Dr. Albert Schweitzer's philosophy of the sacredness of all life also has something of that belief.

This spirit is so basic, so elemental, that we find it even in the lives of the lowest of mankind, as will be evident in this story of a Negrito in the Philippine Islands.

In the war days when our little Filipino brothers proved their courage, heroism, and loyalty with such ultimate finality, I was reminded of this Negrito, one of the strangest characters I ever met in my fifty thousand miles of travel around the world.

We were climbing a mountain in the Philippines in

Northern Luzon and had gone through jungle trails for four hours, finally hiking up the mountain to the habitat of a wild tribe of Negritos. They are a diminutive people, resembling our American Negro, but short enough to stand under the armpits of a man of average height. They live in the trees, eat nuts and roots, and hunt with bows and arrows.

They have been called the lowest tribe in mentality on the islands.

It was a terrifically hot day, and we arrived at our destination, the habitat of the Negritos, around two o'clock, having travelled from early dawn to avoid the intense heat.

Contrary to universal advice, I had not worn a sun helmet, and had a severe sunstroke just before we arrived at the top of the mountain. I was quite ill, and was forced to lie down in the shade of a tree while the others in our party ate the first meal of the day. I could not eat, but watched the others as they ate a picnic lunch, and also watched a circle of naked Negritos hunched down on their bottoms to stare at the Americans, too close for comfort, for they were a dirty lot.

About fifty of these unwashed, diminutive people watched every bite of food that the members of our party put into their mouths, and you could literally see those underfed natives drool as dogs often do when they see food.

As our party ate, the Negritos crowded closer and closer, the circle closing in on the whites until they could almost touch them. One hideous old man was in the forefront of the circle. His repulsiveness made me nauseated when I looked his way. A streak of sunlight coming through the thick trees played across his face with ruthless severity, making the wrinkles, sores, and dirt show up all the more vividly. His body was covered with grey hairs, matted into the scabs and dirt. He was the most repulsive creature I had ever seen in all my travels.

"That old codger represents the nearest thing to an animal that the human being can reach," remarked one of the missionaries who was with us.

"You're right," I agreed. "He has the appearance of a Borneo orangutan, except that he is smaller."

"He lives like an orangutan—up in a tree in his nest of matted palm branches and grass," replied another missionary, who now and then visited these isolated Negritos.

"I've travelled among most of the wild tribes of the world all my life, and I have seen the lowest humans on earth, in Africa, South America, Malaysia, Borneo, Java, and Australia. I have never seen a type so low in the human scale as that old man," continued a photographer who had covered the earth in his time.

We discussed the old Negrito as we rested, I trying to take some nourishment in order to regain strength to return through the mountain jungle trail to the valley below, where our train had halted.

The old man did not know that we were discussing him, for he could not understand our language. He did not know that we "wise" whites had consigned him to the lowest rung on the ladder of humanity. He stared at us, now and then turning his eyes from those who ate to watch me as I lay on the ground weak from illness.

One of our group, a philosopher, who was always proving something, it seemed, remarked, "That man is not even a human being. I think I could prove that he is even lower down than the human scale. He doesn't seem to me to have a single spark of humanity left in him!" That was the decision of our wise and sophisticated, well-fed group of whites, and the decision might have remained at that unanimously if it hadn't been for the fact that the old Negrito didn't appear to understand our talk and therefore didn't live up to our conclusions. He upset the apple-cart of our ultimate white wisdom!

When we had finished our luncheon, the missionaries started to hand out what was left of the food to those emaciated, starving men, women, and children. The old man, whom we had described as the lowest type of human being we had ever been in contact with, seemed, after all, to be the leader of that tribe, partly because of his age—perhaps more because of something which we were soon to discover.

A missionary handed him the first sandwich because he looked to be the oldest and the hungriest.

Did he eat it himself? He did not. He handed it to a child standing near him.

Another sandwich was handed to him. Did that old man whom we had decided was more animal than human eat that sandwich? He did not. He took it over behind a tree, where another grisly Negrito, even older-appearing, was hunched on the ground, shyly peering around the palm tree, and gave it to him.

A third sandwich was handed to him. Did he eat it? He did not. He presented it to an old woman near by. And so it continued, until the last bit of food was disposed of.

"It may be that he is not hungry," someone said.

"And it may be that he is generous, sacrificial, and kindly," was the reply of a woman in our party.

Then I noticed that the old man had disappeared. In a few moments he returned, carrying an armful of big broad palm leaves. He spread the leaves out on the ground under the shadiest tree, did that old man—that hideous-looking monster—and motioned in unmistakable gestures of kindliness for me to roll over and lie down on the bed he had made for me. He had noticed that I was ill. As I rolled over, a few tears rolled down my cheeks at the same time, partly from weakness, partly for another reason.

Again he disappeared, and when he returned he was carrying a big bamboo tube of clear water slung over his scrawny shoulders. He brought it to where I was lying on the bed of palm leaves he had laid for me. Then, with a quick shrug of his shoulder he swung the bamboo tube, somewhat like an American soda jerk throws an ice cream drink from his glass, and over my head and face I felt the cool refreshment of spring water, the first I had had in that day of intense heat. From the tube he poured some water into what looked to be a wild gourd cup and gave it to me to drink, did that old man whom we, in our infinite white wisdom, had decided was the lowest type of human being we had ever seen on earth. Yet in that kindly service I could hear faintly echoed: "Whosoever shall give you a cup of cold water in my name, I say unto you he shall not lose his reward."

In this simple story is my way of saying that I have never seen a cup of cold water given in His name, in the name of humanity, to anybody, anywhere, at any time, which had in it more of the spark of God than I saw that hot tropical afternoon. That native of the Philippines is one of the most unforgettable characters I have ever met. I often think of him and his kind as I hear first-hand sto-

ries of courage during the war, even unto death, and remember the heroism these little brown brothers of ours
demonstrated during the invasion of the Philippines by
the Japanese.

IX

A KOREAN JOAN OF ARC

IT IS NATURAL for us to think of all missionaries as illus-
trating Christian service in their own lives. It is the very
essence of the meaning of missionary work, but it is heartening and inspiring to know that that spirit carries over
from the missionaries to their converts, as it does in this
dramatic human interest story of Induk Pak, a Korean
Joan d'Arc.

I first met Induk Pak in the West Gate Prison in Seoul,
Korea, in 1919.

She was one of a half-dozen girls from the Methodist
schools in Seoul who had been arrested and thrown into
prison, in what I then thought, and still think, was a
ruthless, barbarian manner. At least one of the girls was
beaten to death.

It was all because of the Korean Independence Movement. Japan had taken over Korea, in typical Japanese
fashion, by right of superior power and intrigue. I happened to be in Korea at that time. There was a mass meeting of the Korean Independence Movement in a field
outside of Seoul. These Korean girls, cultured, educated,
beautiful of form and face, full of spirit, attended that
meeting.

The Japanese gendarmes came one night (they usually
made such arrests by night) to the doors of our girls' school

and demanded these girls whose names they had with them.

But of all the girls who were arrested, Miss Pak was given special treatment. The other girls were put in solitary confinement, and were almost starved for six months, one of them was beaten to death. Visitors were not permitted. All books and most of the girls' clothing were taken from them, but Miss Pak was spared all this for a peculiar reason. The Japanese wanted what they called "a model prisoner" to show off to foreign visitors. Induk Pak was called that model prisoner; a clean, warm room and good food were given her, and she was permitted to have her Bible. And it was she who was shown to visitors from foreign lands when they came to visit the terrible West Gate Prison in which were imprisoned the political offenders. I was among the interested foreign visitors who went to the prison in 1919.

But now we shall jump back a few years to get Induk Pak's "Believe-It-or-Not" story, because it just happens to be one of the most bewildering, improbable stories it has ever been my privilege to hear.

Her father was a Chinese scholar, who took the Royal Examination three times, and passed it in Seoul. The last time that stately old Korean father took his examination he walked one hundred and eighty miles over the Black Diamond mountain range, taking ten days each way to complete each journey. When we think of Induk's dignified old father, we come to understand the eager search for education, the courage, and the fortitude of this frail, slant-eyed, brown-skinned, beautiful Korean girl, who literally thrilled thousands of people in churches all over the United States with the story of her life and the even more exciting and appealing story of her movement to establish co-operatives in the country districts of Korea for Korean women. This happened in a country where it is the custom that women should be seen and not heard, that they should remain humbly in the background and never seek an education. In the first part of this century, it was a positively unheard-of thing for a Korean girl even to think of wanting an education, and it was, therefore, a very daring thing for this girl to decide that, though all the powers that be were arrayed against her, she was determined to get one.

It was not only her old scholarly father who planted this seed in her soul, the missionaries from America came along with the same ridiculous idea and ideal: that women had as much right to an education as men. Induk Pak's mother said, "If they won't give girls a chance for an education, I'll make a boy out of her. I'll train her to act and think and play and dress and live like a boy."

For a year that audacious mother did just that. She trained her daughter to act, think, and live like a boy. She had her daring plan, one of the most unheard-of procedures in human history.

There were no schools for girls anywhere in Korea. So her brave and determined mother decided to dress Induk Pak as a boy and send her to a boys' school. In order to do that it was necessary that she and her mother move to another village where they were not known, for, of course, they could not get by with any such unprecedented social rebellion and deception as that in their home village. The whole family moved to a village about a hundred miles away. Induk Pak was in boy's clothing, which she wore on the long overland journey, every step of it on foot, as her father before her had taken his journey for the Royal Examinations. The mother even changed her name to that of a boy.

When Induk Pak told me about her first day in school, she said, "I shall never forget my first day in a boys' school, dressed as a boy. My mother had told me: 'Remember, you're a boy—not a girl. Remember that a boy can sit anywhere he pleases—any way he pleases.' That suited me, for I always did like to sit crosslegged on the floor. In Korea, the one who reads loudest in school, gets the first prize, and, believe me, [she had learned American slang] I got first prize, for I loved to yell like a boy. I learned to climb trees, to climb to the eaves of the houses to gather birds' eggs as Korean boys did, to spin a top, to run races, to jump rope, and to fly kites. Flying a kite—that was a most wonderful joy. The boys made their own kites, with a square boxlike design and no tail. I made my own kite. I played football and competed with fifteen-year-old boys. I was only nine years old. I joined a Sunday school for boys in the village church.

"Then, when I had attended school for two years, the first school in Korea for girls was started by some missionaries. My mother said, 'I think you'd better go to the girls' school now.'

"When I went to say good-by to my teacher and told her I was a girl she said: 'I can't believe it. Are you really a girl?' It was a terrible scandal in the village, for girls were not allowed in the same room with boys, and even grown-up women were never permitted to eat at the same table with the men—even with their own husbands and sons."

Following Induk Pak's grammar-school experience, when

she dressed and lived as a boy in order to get the start of her education, she and her mother decided that she should enter Ewha (meaning Pear Blossom), a Methodist girls' school in Seoul. They did not know that they should take the precaution of writing to see if the school would take her. By weaving much cotton cloth, the mother was finally able to save $1.50 for the train fare to Seoul. Induk Pak was put on a train for the girls' school, and of her experience she told me: "I had never been on a train in my life before and it was an exciting journey. It rained all day long but I didn't care. I had never seen electric light until that journey; I couldn't figure out where the light went when it was turned off. They told me a man named Edison had invented that light. From that minute on I wanted to meet the inventor, and on my first trip to America I went to Fort Meyer and met the great man and inspected the laboratory.

"The next day I went to the school in Seoul. When the principal of the school came to the door I was speechless, for I had never in my life seen a fair, blue-eyed, blonde woman. She looked to me like a princess. I could not believe my eyes—that there were fair-skinned, blue-eyed girls in the world. It was like discovering a new continent to me, and I just stood there with my little bundle of clothing, containing all my worldly possessions, and stared at the principal.

"She smiled down at me and said, 'What do you want?'

"I said, 'I have come to go to school here.'

" 'But who is your sponsor?'

"I didn't know what a sponsor was, but when I caught the general idea I replied, 'I have none.'

" 'Have you any money?' she asked.

"I showed her the ninety cents I had left, and said, 'Teacher, I have ninety cents. My mother paid my way on the train, and gave me more than a dollar to spend on the way. And I have saved ninety cents to go to school.' That seemed like a fortune to me, for I had never seen even that much money before in all my life. It was colossal." (I loved her American vocabulary—it also was colossal.)

" 'But we haven't room for you, child. We are over-crowded now,' said the teacher of the Mission school.

" 'Can't I sleep on the floor? Haven't you just one little corner in which I could lie down at night? I have always slept on the floor. I don't need a mat to sleep on and I'll keep out of the way and won't go to sleep until all of the girls are in bed.' She answered, 'Yes, we could find a place for you to sleep, but we haven't enough food to take care of another girl.'

" 'But,' I replied, 'don't the other girls ever leave anything, pieces of bread, scraps—rice? I could eat what the other girls leave behind and don't eat. I won't eat much, lady. I'm not used to eating much, lady. Just what a bird eats, that's all!'

"My eager determination evidently won her heart for she took me in, even though the school was overcrowded, and there I stayed working my way until I graduated—and later became its principal."

Induk Pak never forgot that electric light she first saw on her first train ride going to Seoul—and she never forgot the man who invented it. During her four years in the Missionary School for Girls in Seoul she learned to speak English, read stories and illustrations—learned American ways and the spirit of America through her teachers, the idea of freedom for women as it was lived in the United

States, and wanted finally to get to America more than she had ever wanted anything else in all her life, even more than she had wanted an education.

And what can stop a beautiful, attractive, smiling, vivacious young woman who in her girlhood had been willing to disguise herself as a boy for two years in order to get an education? The answer is: Nothing can stop such a personality, and nothing has.

One day, a blind man named C. G. Steinhart of Wilmington, Illinois, heard about Induk Pak. He wrote to the school authorities that he was so moved by her courage and daring that he would send her five dollars a month for seven years to help further her educational ambition. But let Induk Pak tell it herself:

"I prayed for six years that I might get to America and see my benefactor. I heard of Wesleyan College in Macon, Georgia, and I wrote to them and told them my story. That was the same school from which Madame Sun Yat Sen graduated when she was Li Soong, wife of the first president of the Chinese Republic. They let me come. I spent two years there, from 1926 to 1928. I wanted an A.B. I didn't know what an A. B. meant when I landed in the United States. I talked to God, and I said to Him: 'God, you've just got to open up the way for me to get through and get an A.B.—and He did. He did it in various ways. He always has various ways to help, I find. People gave me gifts. I went about among the churches of the South and told my story. In 1927, I wanted to go to the Student Volunteers' Convention in Detroit. It cost seventy-five dollars. I didn't have seven dollars. But it came. It always did. It always does if you pray and trust and work. I spoke at that convention on 'What Does Christ

Mean to me?' And, believe me, [some more American slang] He meant a lot to me—He meant everything I had become. He meant getting me to the United States—everything. He was—what you call it in your song—'He was My Everything.'

"In February, the Field Secretary of the Student Volunteer Movement invited me to travel for them through the colleges. The first place I spoke was in Gettysburg. When I learned that I was to go there I cried out with joy. I went to Gettysburg, climbed the picket fence surrounding the spot where Lincoln delivered his Gettysburg Address, climbed that alone (I had learned to climb like a boy, you will remember), skirts and all, much to the chagrin of my escort; climbed that eight-foot iron fence, stood on the spot where Lincoln had spoken, and proclaimed his very address, which I had learned in the Mission school in Seoul. In 1928 and 1929 I spoke in 205 colleges in America to more than 200,000 students, telling them my story. I got my coveted A.B. degree from Wesleyan College at Macon, Georgia, and then went to Columbia in New York for my M.A. I went to Great Britain and Ireland in 1931 for three months, then to Belgium, to India, where I spoke to three hundred men students—not another woman there in Lucknow University. I have travelled in thirty-two countries, absolutely alone, during the last ten years, and never, anywhere, have I been molested.

"Then I went back to Korea and studied the condition of Korean women in the rural regions, soon found that they could not get along without me, nor could I get along without them, so I wrote a book on it. There we organised 'The Society for Work Among Korean Women.'

"They had absolutely nothing, those rural Korean

women. At first we met in dugouts in the earth—and we had to meet secretly. Then I organised what we called a Consumer's Co-operative among the women. Each woman saved fifteen cents a month. We used that as capital. The women bought and sold the products which they had made in their homes. Women could make money only in limited ways. We would buy a pig for a woman. She would raise it until it had a litter of little pigs. Then our Co-operative would sell her pigs for her and she would raise some more. Then she would pay back the ten dollars that her pig cost, and at the end of the year we would pay ten per cent interest to the members of our Woman's Rural Co-operative League. That was the only way we could save those poor women from the sharks, money-lenders, and middle men. But there was a more important objective than just helping them with their economic problems. That was but a means to an end. The co-operative movement gave us a change to get into their homes to talk with them, to liberate them from their age-old bondage to their men, to give them ideas of freedom, their right to live free lives and to break away from the dominance of men; to teach them about Christ and His attitude toward women. That was our objective, but the co-operative movement among rural women in Korea had grown so fast that I went back there to head it up, build little villages near Seoul, villages with ten or fifteen cottages in them, so that the uneducated rural women of Korea may come nearer to a city and get into its schools, culture, and religion. This will give them courage and self-reliance. It will help them to break away from their bonds of many centuries."

Now that the war is over and Induk Pak has survived it —though her Co-operative League did not survive—it is interesting to note that she has become one of the truly great personalities of Korea, indeed, of the world.

During World War II Miss Pak was under the constant sharp scrutiny of the Japanese police, was thrown into prison several times because the Japanese Army knew very well that her sympathies were with her own Korean people and with the American Army.

Since the war she has been brought back to this country four times by our Government, has had conferences with President Truman and General Marshall in the State Department because she knows more about the needs of her people and spirit of American democracy than any other woman in Korea.

Induk Pak is held in the same position of high esteem by Koreans as was Madame Chiang Kai-shek by her people in China. Induk Pak still is a liaison officer between her people and this nation.

While in the last stages of writing this book, we had the honor of entertaining Induk Pak in our home. We spent an evening discussing the thesis of this book with her as it applies to her own life, to Korea, and the Korean people. At that time she was in America at the earnest solcitation of Lieutenant-General John Hodge, who was then Commander of our Occupational Army in Korea. The General explained to her, "I do not want you to go back to America as my personal representative, or as representing the Army, but I feel that a woman with your understanding of both the Korean language and the English language, and with your devotion to democracy, should give up everything and go—at once!"

"But," replied Miss Pak, my co-operative farms, my pigs and cows that were butchered for meat by the Japanese!

I feel I must rebuild the Co-operative movement in Korea, that I must stay here and teach the women of Korea, who now have the vote, spirit, and techniques of democracy."

"That can come later. I'll help you in that. Just now you *must* go to the States to best serve the cause of Christianity, democracy and the future of the missionary movement. Just now you must give your time, talents, and personality to interpreting your people and our aims to America. I, personally, want you to go, even though I dare not finance your passage, or have anything to do with your going, because you would then be looked upon as my personal representative or as a voice of the Army of Occupation in Korea."

"Then I must finance this trip myself, General Hodge? Is that your idea?"

"I am afraid that that is the way it must be. I am sorry but that is the way it must be."

"And let my Co-operative movement wait?"

"That is it, Induk Pak," replied the General, sadly—but wistfully.

The fine Christian woman, a product of Christian missions in Korea, a graduate of our Christian schools, sat in silence for a few moments and then looked up to say, "I'll go, General Hodge. I learned in the Christian missionary schools that my time, talents, and life belong to God and humanity. That is what the Christian missionaries have taught me. I shall go. 'Here am I, send me!' When do I start?"

"You start tomorrow morning. I shall arrange a plane for you!"

"But my daughters, my work, my clothes, my husband!"

The General smiled and replied, " 'Here am I, send

me!' means *now,* Induk Pak. There is no time to be lost in delay. The plane will be ready tomorrow morning at seven."

"I'll be ready, General Hodge. I don't know how, but I'll be ready!"

And Induk Pak *was* ready. The big four-motored plane lifted from Korean soil and sailed out through a heavy fog across the Pacific with a single woman passenger on board, a frail, shy, porcelain-like but vigorous, smiling, hopeful, valiant woman: Korea's modern Joan of Arc.

At the time of writing this chapter she has been in America for three months. She has accomplished her diplomatic mission with the President and State Department in Washington, she has spoken all over this nation to hundreds of thousands of Christian people, has been presented with more than one hundred cows for her Co-operative Farms in Korea [she names each cow for the person who presented the cow to her]; and by the time this book is published, she will have returned to Korea and entered into one of the greatest programs that the dawn of a new day has witnessed.

X

"FRED PYKE IS BACK!"

No BOOK ON Christian living would be complete without an illustration from the life of some individual missionary personality. Any man who knows the church could cite a thousand such personalities. I myself, who have travelled around the world visiting the mission fields, could write an entire book on the spirit of serving, sharing, and sacrificing among missionaries, but I select this particular story because it is contemporary, and because it came to its full dramatic climax in the recent World War and will serve as a symbol of service among all missionaries and in all of our fields.

"Fred Pyke is back! Fred Pyke is back!" I heard the word from lip and letter all around the church world, for Fred Pyke had grown to be a missionary legend in the war years. His story is an epic of courage, sacrifice, and service.

The Methodist Missionary Board had ordered all missionaries out of China, for the Japanese were hammering at the very walls of Peking. It was inevitable that they would take Peking within a month. But the rumour came seeping through that Fred Pyke and his Wellesley graduate wife, Frances, had stubbornly taken their stand and would not leave China.

I was interested in this historic drama of missionary courage because I had been in theological seminary with

Fred Pyke around 1910. Fred excelled in track work while a student, and was a Phi Beta Kappa. He took his M.A. and S.T.B. at Harvard after studying at Boston University School of Theology. He was tall, dark, and good-looking, smartly dressed, a Beau Brummel among the students. His eloquence could have placed him in any pulpit in the nation. But, much to the surprise of all of us, Fred Pyke and his wife decided that they would go to China as missionaries.

"The guy is crazy. He could go to any city church in America," was the way one student put it.

"He'll waste his eloquence out there. He could really *be* something if he had sense enough to stay in America and preach," was the unanimous opinion of his fellow students.

"That man has everything, musical ability, education, eloquence, good looks, affable personality, and there he goes, wasting his ministerial sweetness on the desert air of China," one room-mate said.

Thirty-seven years passed, and Fred Pyke and his charming wife dropped into obscurity, so far as the American church world was concerned. Then, as though the ocean had opened and swallowed them, and as if their ship to China had sunk and left no trace, this couple disappeared. During those years many of Fred Pyke's fellow students followed the church routine and were occupying the great churches of his denomination. One or two of them were elected bishops. Still, nothing was heard of Fred Pyke. He had quietly and completely slid down into obscurity. That is, until a few years ago, when the Japanese were threatening China, and particularly Peking. Then his name began to be bandied about dramatically and mysteriously along the grapevine of secret communications throughout the church world. "Fred Pyke is back! Fred Pyke is back!" was heard on every side.

And why did Fred Pyke's name suddenly take on this new romance and drama? It was a simple story, such a story as now and then sweeps the church world when a Sepoy rebellion or a Boxer uprising turns up names and personalities which become legendary figures in the church and missionary World for half a century. The missionary movement has many such stories.

"Fred Pyke is back! Fred Pyke is back!" One heard it on every hand where preachers, missionaries, and church people were gathered. The phrase was spoken in hushed tones, almost reverently—always with profound respect. The story became the outstanding story of missionary courage and sacrifice in the Second World War.

For months the phrase, "Fred Pyke is back," had been intriguing me, because he had been a fellow student of mine, as I have said, in Boston University School of Theology, and I had remembered so well what an impression his going to China had made on all of us. Therefore, I was both startled and pleased one morning in an upper New York State city to pick up the morning newspaper and read that Fred Pyke, one of the heroes of World War II (those were the very words of the newspaper) was to speak that night at a church rally in a local church.

Taking a cab, I went to the church and sat in a back pew. The crowd gathered until the church was packed with eager, excited people.

There were only two men on the platform. One was a rather stout, well-fed looking official, who seemed to be presiding, and, of course, I knew that he must be the

bishop, for he looked so contented, smiling, sure of himself, and heavy-jowled.

There was another man on the platform: small, hollow-
eyed, emaciated, grey of hair, and so feeble-looking that
he seemed to sink far into the big chair, until he looked
like a starved European child refugee.

A feeling of disappointment came over me, for I believed that the Fred Pyke who was on the program had
been delayed, and I had looked forward to a friendly reunion after forty years of separation. I was about to pick
up my hat and go back to my hotel.

Then the bishop arose and began to talk. It was a much
too-long introduction, but finally he said, "And here is Mr.
Pyke." It was Fred Pyke, whose hair, which once had been
black, was now white, whose body, which once had been
robust and athletic, was now emaciated, and whose eyes,
which once had been bright and eager, were now hollow.
He was an old man before his time. With my own full-fed
and comfortable look, I intuitively tried to shrink down
into my seat. I was so ashamed of myself. I wondered
whether the bishop felt the same way.

Then that little old man, in language as simple as a
child's, told his story. He seemed not to be aware that he
was telling us a story which would become one of the immortal legends of the war and of missionary tradition. He
was straightforward, without boasting, and here is his
story, some of it collected that night in Fred's public re-
port, more of it from him personally after that unforgettable night; even more from Chinese friends, missionary
workers and officials:

Long since, the missionary officials of the Methodist
Church had ordered all missionaries out of China, in

which they probably were right. They had gone over the matter carefully, and their decision was to evacuate all missionaries from Japan, China, the Philippines, and Singapore. Those orders had been officially issued. But one missionary, named Fred Pyke, and his wife, Frances, had not obeyed those orders. They had refused to leave, and the officials in New York were very worried about them.

This so-called stubbornness was not entirely unprecedented in missionary annals, for Tyler Thompson did the same thing in Singapore, just before the Japanese bombed the water supply on the hill above the city and were threatening to take the city within a week. It had been done before—in other wars and in other years—namely in the Boxer uprising, but this certainly did throw a monkey wrench into the well-laid plans of the Methodist Board.

Fred Pyke had received a secret telephone call from the native Chinese bishop, who asked that he meet him at his home in Peking. Fred went at once. He knew what was coming. The Chinese bishop was going to try persuasion on Fred Pyke to compel him to evacuate. Fred loved the bishop and respected him.

He entered the room. "Fred, I asked you to come in order to beg you to leave China. You and your wife will be killed within a month if you remain behind. The Board has ordered all missionaries to leave at once, and if you wait another day the ship will have sailed, and then you can't get out before the Japanese enter the city. I beg you to go."

"I'm sorry, Bishop, but we are not going! Frances and I have talked it over and thought it through. We shall not leave!"

"But you will be killed, Fred."

"That may be true, but we'll take our chances. We are not going to invest thirty years in missionary work with these people and then desert them in the hour of their greatest need."

"They will understand. I mean *we* will understand. Nobody will criticise you. It is your right. It is your duty to leave."

"No, it is our duty to *stay*, Bishop, begging your pardon."

"It is not demanded of you, Fred!"

"But my spirit—I mean our spirit—demands it of us. No, we have made up our minds and we are going to stay with our Chinese people. They need us."

"But what can you *do* if you stay? The Japanese will not permit you to *do* anything. They will put you in an internment camp. In fact, that is bound to happen."

"That may be true, but the very fact that we remained and that there are Americans in or near Peking will give our Chinese faith and hope, even though we are in prison."

"Is that your final word, Fred?" asked the Chinese bishop.

"That is our final, well thought-out and prayed-about word, Bishop. I dislike to disobey you, but that is what we feel we must do—stay with our people."

There was a moment of tense silence, and then the bishop took Fred Pyke warmly by the hand as he said, "Fred, that is what I *wanted* you to say and do! That is what I prayed that you would do; but it was my duty as your bishop to order you to leave! Thank God, you are staying!"

Within a short time the Japanese were in Peking; within weeks, the Pykes, along with two thousand other

Americans and English, were interned in a camp not far from Peking.

Almost immediately the Japanese Army put Fred Pyke, the cultured, American college graduate who had seen service for thirty years in China, to work cleaning out the latrines in the camp. It was a vile, disease-ridden task, dangerous every hour of the day—but Fred Pyke did it.

Another missionary friend said to me: "The Japanese figured that if they put this long-time leader of the Chinese to work in this degrading labor he would lose face with his Chinese followers—and losing face is the ultimate calamity in the Oriental world. The task that was given Fred Pyke was the most menial, despicable work the Japanese could conceive for him. They figured that Fred Pyke's influence on the Chinese people would be ended, not only for the period of the war but for all time."

"Did it work?" I asked the missionary.

"What would be your American guess as to whether it worked?"

"Well, *did* it?" I asked again.

"Not only their indignities didn't work, but the very fact that Fred did that vile job for two whole years without complaint, but with a smile, a joke, and in good humour, made him a hero, even to the Japanese police who were supposed to see that he did his work. Even they respected him, and, when Fred comes back to China a hero and a tradition, he will finish his missionary work, and the tradition will grow with the years."

In a torrent of talk, the missionary went on:

"Those Japanese were always miscalculating our American psychology. They first of all miscalculated in assuming that we're too fat and easy-living to fight. They miscalculated again in their assumption that we wouldn't cross the Pacific to bring justice to pass, that we might fight at home and on our own shores but that we would never leave home to fight. Another miscalculation they made has to do with the Christian religion that we have been teaching the Orient for one hundred years, something that is at the very heart of this story of face saving and face losing."

"And what is that?" I questioned.

"They had forgotten entirely the story of another man in the long, long ago, who, one never to-be-forgotten morning walked into a room with His disciples, threw aside His outer garments, dressed Himself in the loin cloth of a slave, and kneeled down before them and washed their feet in order to dramatize for them the greatest teaching of His life, that he who serves another, even in the most menial capacity, becomes automatically the greatest in the Kingdom of God."

After a pause, the missionary continued, "What do *you* think about Fred Pyke losing face because he cleaned out the latrines in the camp? Do even *you* think he would lose face like the Japanese military thought he would?"

"I'll say he wouldn't," I replied, slipping back into the American slang for emphasis.

"And he didn't! When he returns to China he will get a glorious reception! And even the Japanese, especially the Christians, will feel the same way about him and about what he did. I'll say (adopting my own phrase) he didn't, and he will not 'lose face.' Fred 'saved face' the Christian way."

XI

"A SORCERER OF SONG"

BACK IN THE dim years when Edwin Markham was seventeen years of age, an itinerant teacher came to the Suisan hills of California and taught for about two months in a country school, and then, as was the custom in those days, went on to other schools on other highways. But he left behind him a young boy who had learned to love the beautiful in color, form and poetry. Edwin Markham was never the same boy after meeting that teacher.

The teacher, one Harry G. Hill, introduced Markham to Tennyson and Bryant, and as Mr. Markham later said of him: "For two or three months I came under the magic spell of Harry G. Hill, a teacher who loved great poetry and who taught me to love it also. This beloved teacher left his mark upon my life. Joy and victory attend him on the long roads ahead."

I had known Edwin Markham twenty-five years and during those years we never sat down to talk together in an intimate mood that he did not refer to Harry G. Hill, his old teacher, whom he always called, "The Enchanter." Then, after talking about that teacher for hours at a stretch, he would always wind up by saying: "And some day I am going to write a poem about him. Education is the most vital thing in life, and, in the final analysis education is not a group of buildings, a salaried faculty, great libraries, or great endowments; education is a teacher,

87

just a great personality who is able to convey his enthusiasm for life, religion, and books to a student. Education is contagious personality."

And sure enough, after hearing him talk of "The Enchanter" for twenty years, finally, the poet did produce that tribute to his old teacher who had taught him only for a few months but when he went on, left behind him a poet. The poem appears in Markham's *Eighty Songs at Eighty*:

> "It was far in the west by a lonely road,
>   Dusty and grey and long,
> When suddenly into the schoolhouse strode
>   A sorcerer of song.

> "He opened to us the lyric doors
>   Of the deeper world that waits,
> Throbbing behind our skies and shores,
>   Pulsing through lives and fates.

> "He read from a poet of golden rhyme,
>   Who mourns the dying years,
> Who pours the eternal pain of time
>   Into his song of tears.

> "He read to us all from the great of old,
>   From the shining poet clan,
> Who bring again the Age of Gold,
>   When youth and wonder ran.

> "And, as the vibrant verses flew
>   Impassioned from his tongue,
> He seemed to change; his sad face grew
>   Mysteriously young.

> "He walked as one whose heart is held
>   By some long look ahead,
> As one who sees the great of eld,
>   The dead who are not dead.

"And when he was too stirred to speak,
        He turned a wistful eye
As if instinctively to seek
        Some signal from the sky.

"Sometimes he paused as if he heard
        Strange music in the air—
As if some Vision of the Word
        Hung a bright moment there."

Then Harry G. Hill disappeared from the Suisan Hills
never to come again, and the poet ponders on "The Enchanter":

"I wonder now what place he fills
        In what high-heart romance;
I'm sure he's on melodious hills
        And where the children dance.

"And when God passes, he must pause
        And hark with deep regard
To hear him plead the poet's cause:
        For God too is a bard."

Perhaps no more beautiful tribute was ever penned to
a teacher than that, and yet Arthur Guiterman's "Education" from *Death and General Putnam,* which I quote by
special permission of the author and publishers, is a close
rival of Mr. Markham's *The Enchanter,* because it sums
up the same spirit of education:

"Mark Hopkins sat on one end of a log
        And a farm boy sat on the other.
Mark Hopkins came as a pedagogue
        And taught as an elder brother.
I don't care what Mark Hopkins taught,
If his Latin was small and his Greek was naught,
For the farmer boy he thought, thought he,
        All through lecture time and quiz,

'The kind of a man I mean to be
Is the kind of a man Mark Hopkins is!'

"Theology, languages, medicine, law,
Are peacock feathers to deck the daw
If the boys who come from your splendid schools
Are well trained sharpers or flippant fools.
You may boast of your age and your ivied walls,
Your great endowments, your marble halls,
    And all your modern features.
Your vast curriculum's scope and reach
And the multifarious *things* you teach—
    But what about your teachers?
Are they men who can stand in a father's place,
Who are paid, best paid, by the ardent face
When boyhood gives as boyhood can,
Its love and faith to a fine true man?

"No printed word or spoken plea
Can teach young hearts what men should be,
Not all the books on all the shelves,
But what the teachers are themselves.
For education is, Making Men;
So is it now, so was it when
Mark Hopkins sat on one end of the log
And James Garfield sat on the other."

President James A. Garfield, in an address before the
alumni of Williams College in 1871, said, "I am not willing that this discussion should close without mention of
the value of a true teacher. Give me a log hut with only a
simple bench, Mark Hopkins on one end, I on the other,
and you may have all the buildings, apparatus and libraries without him." Mark Hopkins was President of
Williams College from 1836 to 1872, and it is interesting
to note that Garfield's own son, Harry A. Garfield, also

became president of the same college some forty years later.

I am glad that Guiterman entitled his poem just plain "Education." He might have selected a more poetic title but he could never have selected a more pregnant word to encompass the meaning of the thing he wanted to say, that education consists of a boy and a teacher in whatever surroundings they happen to find themselves.

In recent years we have had autobiographies and biographies of teachers of the same type that these two poets describe. I have a little one-foot shelf of them in my library, and I turn to them frequently for inspiration. The first is *Alice Palmer,* the second president of Wellesley College, a book written about this woman's passion for personalities and her love for her students, by Dr. George Herbert Palmer, her husband, who was a great teacher himself at Harvard. It is one of the truly great books of our American literature.

A second great book about teaching is Rolla Walter Brown's *Dean Briggs,* a fascinating tale of an unorthodox teacher who had a supreme scorn for Ph.D.'s, but who had a great reverence for the personalities of his students, a man who made an unforgettable impression on his students and who will be remembered at Harvard longer than most teachers for that reason. Rolla Brown says of Dean Briggs:

"Instead of driving men through a period of discipline enforced by all the machinery of systematised education, he set men free and when men experienced any high kind of freedom they begin to discipline themselves. . . .

"For he was a shrewd genius who created creators. . . .

"It was one of his students who once called his type of teaching 'scholarship illuminated by character.' "

This man knew what education meant. It meant the contact of an older man who had knowledge and character with a younger man whom he could love and to whom he could give the contagion of all three—education, love, and character.

The third book in my small library shelf of great teachers is called *And Gladly Teach*, written by Bliss Perry, who, strangely enough, was also a teacher at Williams, as well as at Harvard, and once editor of the *Atlantic Monthly*, but always one who loved his teaching more than any of his literary activities. To read his book one gets a plunge into the cooling stream of a beautiful attitude toward teaching and boys, the same attitude that Edwin Markham's *The Sorcerer of Song* must have had.

The fourth book is Dr. William Lyon Phelps' *My Autobiography*, the rollicking, happy-go-lucky tale of a pioneering prophet in the school of unorthodox teaching which delights the souls of other teachers just as his teaching itself delighted the souls of thousands of young men who had passed through his classrooms.

Here are four great teachers of my day, unforgettable teachers, and all of them, including the two teachers of whom our two poets speak, unorthodox. These were men who had no great awe of advanced degrees, who had a wholesome respect for learning and discipline, but who first of all looked on teaching as an opportunity to make friends with young men and women, a sublime privilege of conveying from one personality to another the great loves and truths and habits of life, men who through love, laughter, and fellowship shed their manifold light down the long pathway that youth has to take.

> "It was out in the west by a lonely road,
>   Dusty and grey and long,
> When suddenly into the schoolhouse strode
>   A sorcerer of song."

We may thank God for the great teachers who have become Sorcerers of Song to thousands of us through all the years behind us; men and women from Grammar school on, who have pushed back the world's horizons for us, who have introduced us to the great of the earth, the novelists, poets, painters, prophets; who have given us a glimpse of "the ancient and beautiful things of life"; who have taken us by the hand and led us to the mountain peaks; who have shown to us sunrises and sunsets, starlit nights, dawns, days, the solar seasons, God and eternity; those who have had the spirit of service in their souls and who have given us a glimpse of what it means to devote their lives to others.

XII

"THE POWER THAT SINGS THROUGH ME"

ONE OF THE most fascinating observations I have made in interviewing great creative personalities is the fact that they all seem to have the spirit of Christian service in their souls.

Mr. Fritz Kreisler has it, and says that none of the money he earns through his music belongs to him, because his music is a gift of God and he is only the steward of that music and that money.

One day in Berlin, Germany, when I was lunching in his very humble home he said to me, "I have never owned a home, because a home would stand between me and all the homeless of the world. I have never eaten a luxurious meal if I could help it, because that meal would stand between me and all the hungry of the world."

Edwin Markham once said to me about his famous Lincoln poem: "I told Chauncey Depew, when he asked me to write it, that I would give it to him if it were given to me. I said that because I have always felt that all of my poems came to and through me, that I had little to do with them, that they were a gift from the Eternal Creative Spirit, and that I was merely a medium through which *He* was speaking. Because of that I have always lived frugally and simply. The money I make from poetry is not mine— but *HIS!*"

Every great creative artist I have known has had that feeling, including Cyrus Dallin, the sculptor; Luther Burbank, the plant creator; Vachel Lindsay, the poet; William Allen White, the editor and novelist, and many others. Roland Hayes, the great Negro baritone, who recently celebrated his thirtieth year on the concert stage with a recital in Symphony Hall, Boston, feels this way, as his story which follows will prove:

"I was born of former slave parents in a Georgia village called Little Ros, later named Curryville—so small and insignificant a village that it is not even mentioned in giographies or noted on maps.

"My father was killed by a falling tree when I was five years old. Mother called in a fine old former Negro slave to help her take care of the fifteen-acre farm which we rented on shares. There were three of us boys, and we all worked on the farm under the direction of the old Negro helper. It was he who told me that my ancestors were tribal leaders on the coast of Africa and that my paternal grandfather had handed down to me something which should make me respect myself and my race.

"In the community where I was born, the hard-working Negroes had the gift of song. Moreover, they were deeply religious. They sang nothing but Negro spirituals. Jazz and the 'blues' were looked upon as profane. The Negroes of that community sang the spirituals with deep devotion, unbounded humility and worship. The Negro did not approach God; he did not attempt to call Him in his song and prayer; he just surrounded God, face averted, with his music.

"When I was twelve years of age, my dear old mother decided that we boys must have an education. She told us

stories about educated men, leaders in all realms of life
who had come to their leadership solely because they had
acquired an education. She said, 'We're goin' somewhere
to get you boys an education!'

A year later we started for Chattanooga in an old wagon.
Mother rode, and we boys walked that sixty miles bare-
footed to save our shoes. As we trudged along, Mother
told us how we would work it out. One of the three must
be at work all the time, but it would not always be just the
same one.

"I got a job in a sash and window factory at three dollars
a day. In a few months I was made foreman of the factory. I always liked to sing, and I think that that was one
of the reasons I was promoted. I sang at my work.

"However, as it turned out, our plan for an education
was knocked to pieces. For I was able to keep my job and
my brothers were not. So I became the sole support of the
family.

"It was not long after arriving in Chattanooga that I
was invited to sing in a church choir. It was in that choir
that I met Mr. Arthur Calhoun, an educated Negro musi-
cian, and was taken to a home where I heard, for the first
time, the voices of Caruso and Melba on phonograph records.

"From that night on, I knew that I was destined for
something which was beyond my comprehension. It was
as if something were calling me from far beyond any hori-
zon I had ever known before. It was like a religious conversion. That night I was born again. I had a sudden and
startling revelation.

"The voices of great singers on a phonograph sealed
my resolution to become a great artist so that purpose

could work through me. A great happiness flooded my soul. It was as if a bell rang in my heart!

"Two years after that experience I decided to go to Nashville, Tennessee, where I entered Fisk University when I was nineteen. Here I became a member of the Fisk Jubilee Singers, and when they went to Boston for a concert I was with them. At the close of that concert, I had a hunch I should remain in Boston.

"I found a job as a bell boy in a hotel and later became a page in the office of the John Hancock Insurance Company.

"Now that I had a regular job, I sent for my mother, and we set up housekeeping in a cheap little apartment where I made our furniture out of packing boxes. I was making only seven dollars a week, but we managed to live.

"My mother was the most wonderful human being I ever knew. I have a sacred shrine in my music room for her. On the wall there is a portrait of her done by a famous Boston artist, Harry Sutton. I keep two vases of flowers, one on each side of it. I change those flowers myself every morning.

"After I had been singing for a few years in Boston, I was invited to New York in 1915 to give a concert at the Music School Settlement. I knew that I never would arrive until I had given a recital in Symphony Hall, Boston.

"But no responsible group would undertake the risk of sponsoring such a recital. So once again I decided to do it myself. I have found that in all the major steps of my life I have had to help myself.

"I planned a recital in Symphony Hall against the advice of all my teachers and friends. I had to guarantee the managers of the hall four hundred dollars. I took the telephone book and selected two thousand names. I tried to pick Back Bay people, who were wealthy and who might become patrons of the concert. I asked them to take tickets at a dollar and fifty cents each, to help me out. I told them in my letters—every one of which I hammered out myself on an old typewriter—just what I was trying to do. I was trying to get a hearing. The answers started coming in at an astonishing speed. The life insurance company where I worked took half of Symphony Hall. It was packed. Seven hundred persons were turned away that night. I cleared two thousand dollars. It was a vindication of my faith in my purpose.

"Shortly after my Symphony Hall recital, I was invited to Santa Monica, California.

"After my concert in Santa Monica a man said to me, 'I have heard all the famous singers. When I listen to you, I get the same things I get from their singing, but I also get something more. What is it?'

"I did not know how to answer that man.

"That night before I went to bed I asked myself what it was he had heard in my singing which he had not heard in the singing of others. Was there really something different that was distinctly mine? If so, what could it be?

"As I lay half asleep, I suddenly arose in my bed and asked myself: 'Can it be something that was given to me by my forebears? Have we Negroes some heritage from the past that is ours alone? Can I help my race to make its contribution to life?'

"I said to myself that night that I would go to Africa, the home of my people, and try to learn the secrets of my race. So, with the money I had made through my Symphony Hall recital in April, 1920, I went to England. But my real destination was Africa.

"When I reached England it was the time of the uprisings in the British possessions, and a man of my color was not very welcome in London. There were long, hard weeks before I could get a hearing. Finally, I was scheduled to give a recital in Wigmore Hall. Everything seemed suddenly to turn against me. My money was gone, and I was likely to be faced with a demand for advance payment on the hall. Tickets were not selling well. If they demanded the advance payment on the hall, as was the custom, I was finished.

"But, fortunately, I had been asked by Dr. Hugh Chapman to sing in the Chapel Royal, where the King and Queen attended church services. There I sang an old spiritual, 'He Never Said a Mumblin' Word.'

"A few weeks after that I was singing at the home of a friend, Stephen Graham, worrying every minute about the demand that might be made on me for the advance rent of Wigmore Hall, and I knew I didn't have a penny. I was haunted every minute by that fear. I was sick with worry. In the middle of that tea, I was called to the phone. My heart sank. Here was the dreaded news I was expecting. I went to the phone. A friend's voice said, 'Have you heard the news?'

"My throat was dry. I could hardly reply, but I managed to choke out the words, 'What news?'

"Then I heard him say like a voice in a fog, 'You are commanded to sing at Buckingham Palace!' The tears ran down my cheeks. I dared not go back to face the people at that tea.

"Two days later, when I went to Buckingham Palace,

the first thing Queen Mary, now the Queen Mother, said to me was, 'I hear you have been singing in our Chapel Royal.'

"Then they took me into a side room and asked me questions for half an hour. I told them of my experience when for the first time I heard phonograph records of Caruso and Melba, and of my conviction that I had a message for the world, and a mission, that mission being to interpret to the world my people at their best.

"The next day Melba sang for the King and Queen, and they asked her if she had ever heard me sing. She had never heard of Roland Hayes, and I did not wonder. Then they told her about me, and suggested that she hunt me up in London and hear me sing.

"Through a mutual friend, Roger Quilton, son of an English earl, she got in touch with me. He planned a party to which he invited Fritz Kreisler, Melba, and half a dozen distinguished musicians.

"That was an eventful meeting for me. I sang before Melba, and she said to me, 'The King and Queen are right! You are truly a great singer!'

"Soon after this I made a European tour. It was at one of my scheduled concerts in Berlin in 1924 that I had a terrifying experience. The French were occupying the Rhine and were policing it with Negro troops. German indignation was running high. I was in Prague. The American Consul there received several letters protesting against my singing in Berlin, asking if an American Negro was to insult the spirit of Goethe, Schiller, and other great writers of Germany by singing plantation songs from the cotton fields of America in Beethoven Hall. The Consul advised me not to go to Berlin. However, I went. On the night of my concert, with my Negro accompanist, I took a closed taxicab to Beethoven Hall.

"I had never had that experience before. But I remembered my mission. I did then what I have always done at the beginning of a concert. It is my habit when I step onto any stage to recall to myself that I am merely an instrument through which my mission is being fulfilled. I stood there with hands clasped before me, praying—praying that Roland Hayes might be entirely blotted out of the picture, that the people sitting there might feel only the spirit of God flowing through melody and rhythm, that racial and national prejudices might be forgotten.

"Usually when I do that sincerely, the audience instinctively feels what is happening as I commune with my Father.

"Beethoven Hall was packed with people. The criticism and newspaper reports had aroused great public interest and indignation over the appearance of an American Negro singer, and I was, for the first time in my life as a concert singer, apprehensive.

"At the appointed time, I walked on the stage with my accompanist. I myself stood in the curve of the piano ready to sing my first number, when a wave of hissing, stomping, and anger swept up at me from that indignant crowd. I stood quietly, awaiting the time when they would vent their spite, racial prejudice, and fury, but, instead of quieting down after a decent interval, the mob spirit got stronger and stronger, until, after five minutes, it seemed to me as if a thousand arrows of hate were being fired into my breast from the audience. I did not know just what to do. My accompanist suggested that we leave the stage and cancel the recital. I didn't want to do that, for that would have admitted defeat and might turn into an international incident.

"As I stood there, praying that their anger would cease and I could go on with my scheduled recital, it seemed to the audience like a gesture of defiance and their anger arose like a torrent of hate flung at me. It seemed about to sweep me from the platform, but I stood there quietly, still praying, hoping and waiting for quiet. But it did not come.

"Then a sudden inspiration came to me and I whispered to my accompanist, without taking my eyes from the angry crowd: 'Get out *This Is My Peace* by Beethoven and I'll sing that as my first number.'

"He found the music and started to play the accompaniment, softly, slowly, tenderly. Suddenly the hissing, stomping, and shouting perceptibly died down. I sang the first verse and a hush fell over the angry crowd. By the time I finished the song you could have heard the fluttering feather from a bird's wing as it touched the earth. The crowd was as hushed as a harp to the sound of God's coming, as the pines to the low wind's humming, as our friend Angela Morgan says.

"From that minute on I found that audience the most responsive audience I have ever sung before. That song had subdued the gathering and I went on to finish my concert, even singing a few French songs which I had originally scheduled.

"When the concert was over the applause and cheering was deafening. For five whole minutes they cheered, almost as long as they had hissed me at the beginning of the concert. They surged onto the stage, got me on their shoulders, and carried me around that great hall. I have never before, or since, had such response or such a tribute.

"It was not the music that did it, although the selection of that number, *This Is My Peace* was a happy choice. It was what was in my heart, my feeling that I was only a pipe for Omnipotence to sound through, that I was there for a great purpose, perhaps an international purpose of good will to bring to that embittered German audience a feeling of brotherhood and comradeship. It had worked. It always does. When an artist feels that his talent is only a stewardship to use for God and humanity he can accomplish miracles with an audience. It has always been so. There is a stewardship of song and talent as surely as there is a stewardship of possessions and things."

"Mr. Hayes, do you accept a stewardship of possessions as well as of talent?" I asked this kindly, gentle, consecrated man.

"Yes, I have always tithed my income. My plan is to use the money in building a great educational institution in my dear old mother's birthplace in Georgia. My plans are incomplete, but my hope is to build a school for Negro children, to build it of white marble, to have in the entrance as a symbol of my mother's spirit a white light glowing night and day. My hope is that the educational institution will not only help my race, allay racial prejudice, but that it will also be an ultimate expression of my philosophy of responsibility and Christian stewardship."

XIII

THE MYSTIC CANDLES

IN SPITE OF war and rumours of war, pestilence, famine, totalitarian states, uncertainty, confusion, violence, and death there is still something kindly, loving, beautiful, and heartening alive in the world these days and Mystic Candles are still aglow. And this is the story of a brave, fine woman who helps to keep them aglow in the hearts of American people, a woman who, strangely enough, has received a chance to do a bit of creative work which has enriched her own life and carried a lot of Christian love and light out into the dark places of many American homes.

Through a literal Gethsemane of suffering, Erna Bilkau, who lost her only child, developed what she calls Mystic Candles. And today, in almost every important shop window, department store and gift shop in America, from coast to coast, those tall, beautiful red, white, bronze candles have become one of the most popular expressions of the Christian spirit. But most people who purchase these Mystic Candles do not know the sad, tragic, and yet triumphant story behind them. It is an almost unbelievable saga of sorrow, devotion, and victorious love, which, at Christmas time, leads us once again to the foot of a manger where a Hebrew mother looked down into the face of the child who set all candles aglow in the darkness of the world.

Erna Bilkau told me her story as we sat in a darkening

room with a wood fire burning and two of her great Mystic Candles aglow on the mantlepiece.

She was born in Russia, and soon after her birth her family moved to Germany, where Erna fell in love with a German boy, and married him. They came to America on their honeymoon, and learned to love America, its people, and, most especially its spirit of hope and freedom. Two years later, when she was separated from her husband by a totalitarian tragedy, she fled to America with her two-year-old son, daring to hope that in this land of refuge she could make her own way.

As she said, "Naturally my child meant everything to me, for I had suffered much. It was because of his health that I went to California. He was all that I had in this strange land. My love for him was almost idolatry. I was able to make a moderate living because I had brought with me from Germany a fine collection of books, antiques, keys, old engravings, with which I opened an antique shop. I was getting along quite well when suddenly Jackie, now thirteen, became seriously ill with a throat infection. I remember once going to his room in the hospital, white with my own grief, and Jackie looked up at me and said, "Mother, you look so white. Why don't you get some rouge and put it on? I don't like you so white-looking!"

What my darling boy did not know was that I had been told that very hour that he could not live.

The shock of Jackie's death almost upset Erna Bilkau's mind. She suffered untold agony, and for months she walked the streets at night looking into the windows of homes where she could see little children sitting with their mothers. And once she saw a boy about Jackie's age kneeling at his mother's knee, saying his evening prayers.

She continued, "After such an experience I would go back to my lonely home and lie half-awake all night listening for his breathing, hearkening for his footsteps coming to my room as I heard them when he was living.

"Friends gave me comfort, but my heart seemed to be breaking. I felt as though I was a lone swimmer, swept out to sea, out, out, far beyond my depth, with a terrific undertow tugging relentlessly at my body.

"Then, in my extremity, I did what millions of other souls have done, I turned to God.

"I knelt down beside my bed as I had so often taught Jackie to do. I put my hands together as a little child would do and prayed: 'O God! Come, enter within me and drive this sorrow from my heart; help me to be brave; give me courage to rise and stand on my feet! O God, I need you so much!"

A great sense of peace, quiet, and courage came to her, and, as she puts it, "It was as though God took me my the hand and led me as if I were a child, led me to a great idea. He led me to a little room where Jackie used to play, and I found myself setting up a crude altar to his memory, with small candles burning on it.

"All day and night I burned those candles, but I soon discovered that most candles I could purchase would not burn long enough, and constantly I had to replace them. Then I remembered certain candle-making secrets of my father's, and I worked for months developing a formula which would make those candles burn for weeks instead of for days, and which, as they burned, would emit a strange mystical glow. They looked like tall alabaster columns with inner lights glowing in them, for my candles burned down the center and did not burn the outer shell."

But this mother's grief was so great that she fell ill and went into a coma. She was alone and unconscious for two days, when her neighbours noticed a light burning in her home. They also heard the dogs barking for food, and fearing that something serious might have happened to her, they broke into the house and found her unconscious. Erna Bilkau was then living in Hollywood, and her neighbours happened to be actors. They took her into their home and nursed her back to health. Naturally, they had seen the altar that she had erected to the memory of her son when they first entered her home and they were attracted by the beauty of the candles on the altar. When she told them how she had developed the formula for the candles they wanted to buy some from her.

"No, they are not for sale. I made them for my son, Jackie. They are too sacred to me to sell," replied Mrs. Bilkau.

Then she continued her strange story: "Across the street lived a young married couple who worked in pictures, and whose names, if I dared to tell them, would be well known to all picture fans. They had been quarrelling for months and were on the verge of a divorce. I learned of their trouble and sent them several of my Mystic Candles for their dining-room table. Shortly after that they came over to visit me and thank me for the candles. They stayed all evening. I told them all about Jackie, whom they had known; what his death had meant to me, and then of how I had tried to temper my grief by making those beautiful candles. Once during their visit I saw tears rolling down the cheeks of the motion-picture wife and I knew that they were not stage tears. I later learned the reason for her tears.

"I learned because she came over to my home the next evening alone. She evidently wanted to tell me something and I waited until it came out naturally. It did a few minutes after her arrival as we sat talking by the light of some candles.

" 'You know, Mrs. Bilkau, when you sent those beautiful candles to us we put them on our table. They looked for all the world like the white alabaster columns of Taj-Mahal in India. Jim and I visited India together and we loved the beautiful story of how the Indian prince had built the Taj-Mahal as a memorial to his wife, whom he loved with a great devotion. Your candles reminded us of the temple and of that love. After dinner we would sit in our living-room, the candles on our mantel, and we'd live and dream over other and happier days. In that darkened room those candles created a mystic glow and hushed our hearts. It seemed incongruous to quarrel in such an atmosphere, and we have been quarrelling so much lately. So we fell into a mood of almost holy quiet. I do not know whether you will understand that or not. I know it sounds somewhat like melodrama, but I want you to know that your candles have saved our home! Last night Jim himself suggested that we come over to thank you for them. I was very happy that he had made the suggestion, and that accounts for our visit of last night.' "

Then came the revelation of the possibilities of the Mystic Candles to Mrs. Bilkau, as she tells it in her own words:

"That woman's experience was a revelation to me. It shook my soul awake. It made me feel as if, after all, there might be something in life for me to do. Perhaps those candles had a mission to humanity. Perhaps the light of my candles would speak peace to troubled souls, give homes and hearts the cathedral touch. Perhaps that was to be my mission in life. It would help to ease the terrible loss in my life. It was an idea that stirred me like a religious conversion. I seemed to be God-guided by that thought. It had worked in one home. Why not in others? So I started to make those Mystic Candles with that thought in mind. Every candle was a prayer and an act of worship with me.

"I worked for months to perfect the candles. Starting with the formula I remembered from my father, I first developed a candle that would burn for weeks. My second problem was to develop a candle that would burn deep down through the center around the wick without burning the sides, so that it would glow with a strange radiance as it burned. I developed candles of all shades and sizes, and this was followed with what I called the Drip Candle.

"Henry Fonda was the first one to buy my candles and he started me on an unexpected business career. He not only bought my candles but he told all of his motion-picture friends of whom I have spoken. My friends told me later that when Henry Fonda came into their homes he would just stand and look at the candles, saying nothing for several minutes. One evening, he said to his friends, 'I must see the woman who makes those candles. I must see her!'

"My friends replied, 'But she is too shy. She won't come over here if she knows you are here, for she is afraid of people, especially celebrities.'

" 'Well, then, we'll fool her!' said Henry Fonda, 'We'll just go over and see her if she won't come to see us.'

"And that," continued Mrs. Bilkau, "is exactly what he

did! I shall never forget the night he came. I heard my doorbell ring and went to the door, nervous and disturbed. When I opened the door, with no further introduction, that kindly man simply said to me, 'Hello, Bilkie, we've come to call on you and to tell you how beautiful your candles are and to see some more of them.'

"That greeting completely captured my heart. When he called me 'Bilkie,' a name by which he has called me ever since that day, and which was my nickname back in Germany, I lost all my feelings of timidity and we had a most happy evening together.

" 'But I don't want to sell them. They are too sacred to me!' I replied.

" 'But you simply must be willing to sell them, for then you can make enough money to make them in large numbers and make that many more people happy with them as you have made us happy. I want some for my mother and father and for all of my friends. I want to hand on this mystic light, for it has hushed my own heart!'

"Henry Fonda sent some candles to his father and mother and several friends that Christmas. His father was ill in bed, and wrote that they had done him more good than medicine. Henry Fonda told all of his picture friends about them. Ann Harding got interested in them, and little Jean Harding used to come over and watch me making them in my study. She was a sweet child, and I loved her. Nils Aster wanted to build me a shop where I could sell them to the general public, but I was afraid of commercialising that thing which was so personal and so sacred to me.

"It was terrific inward struggle, for my friends kept urging me to manufacture and sell my Mystic Candles, but there was always the feeling that such a thing would be sacrilegious. But even in my final decision I seemed to be God-guided.

"I had a woman friend who was in great grief. She had lost her husband and was poverty-stricken. One day it occurred to me to give her the right to sell my candles in order that she could make a living. She was living alone in New York City, and she was also far from her homeland, for she was a Chinese woman. It seemed fitting that I do at least this. She was both a brave and an industrious woman, and soon, with her industry, the demand for my candles was so great that she urged me to leave Hollywood and go to New York City to help her make the candles. In fact, she was swamped with orders from gift shops, large department stores, from homes and from churches. So, still with the one idea of helping her financial problem, I left Hollywood and went to New York City. I have never gone back to Hollywood, not even to close my house and pack my things, for we have been so industriously making the Mystic Candles that we have both been kept busy, along with hundreds of people working in our shops. We now are making literally millions of these Mystic Candles every year. I pour the money that comes to me from them back into my shop in order to make more work for poor people. I do not feel that the money belongs to me. It is merely mine to use for other people. I am just the steward of that money."

I happen to know that this is a true story, and it is really a beautiful story. I have run across many stories in many moons of interviewing unusual people, and was very much impressed. I also happen to know that Mrs. Bilkau has had many offers from big business organisations to exploit her Mystic Candles on a huge commercial scale, but she refused them all. But, in spite of herself and of her ideals, she has not been able to keep this sacred enterprise from growing by leaps and bounds, and recently she has been unable to supply even half the demands for her candles. Those demands come from every city and state in the Union, from South America, from all over the world.

She sat silently for a few minutes and then gave me a parable which haunts me with an unutterable pathos. Suddenly she looked up and said:

"The great tragedy of war always is that the so-called blackouts which came with bombing not only blacked out my candles and their burning; but those blackouts dimmed the lights of cathedrals and home, and the very light of Christmas itself in warring lands. I read a book by H. G. Wells not long ago in which he symbolised what went on in Europe through an experience that came to him in a European cathedral. It seems that Mr. Wells was in a cathedral one evening at dusk. There was no light in the cathedral save seven candles burning near the altar. Suddenly the janitor came in, walked over to the seven-stick candle, and one by one snuffed each light out, and suddenly Mr. Wells found himself in utter, impenetrable, and what he described as almost terrifying, darkness. It was a complete blackout in that dark and gloomy building. Mr. Wells turned that figure into a symbol of that which always happens in a warring world when, one by one, the seven candles of idealism are snuffed out—love, sincerity, kindness, faith, hope, charity and even worship."

I nodded in response to her vivid story. We were both wrapped in silence, in almost terrifying gloom at the thought. Then, in a sudden blaze of light from a log on the fireplace which had rolled over and started a new flame, her face brightened and she said to me, "The lights of liberty, religion, faith, hope, charity, friendship, and home still burn here in America, and I pray God we may keep them burning."

There didn't seem to be anything for me to say after that beautiful statement of faith and hope, so I grasped her hand and we both walked out into the evening darkness. As we looked up into the skiy it seemed a natural thing to say—and I swear I do not now remember who said it—"The stars are still shining."

It will always be true in human life so long as we have devoted women like Mrs. Bilkau who do creative things, and who, out of great suffering, have come to a life of service to humanity. Thank God, there are many millions of them.

They are the hope of humanity, the only hope we have in these turbulent, tumultuous, storm-tossed, uncertain days. It will have to be united in the spirit of this woman, in the light of the Mystic Candles, symbols of vision and brotherhood.

XIV

"HE TITHES DAHLIAS, TULIPS, TIME AND MONEY"

CHRISTIAN SERVICE EXPRESSES itself in innumerable ways, but I have never found a layman in whom the spirit of service and sharing took more forms than in the life of J. B. Ivey, whose Christian activity manifests itself in his love of flowers, children, life, journalism, and his church.

A grey-haired man, who, dressed in his Sunday best, looks much like Ralph Waldo Emerson, was working in his dahlia garden at Lake Junaluska, when a strange accident happened. As he walked up a steep flight of stone steps, his foot slipped and he fell backward.

The painful result was a slight fracture of the skull and a broken finger. He lay there until a neighbour came running up. Seeing that J. B. Ivey's injuries were serious, this man bundled the Dahlia King of the South into an automobile and carried him to the nearest hospital.

When they both walked into the small-town hospital, the girl at the receiving desk looked at them suspiciously. Both had on working clothes and looked like two tramps who had come off a freight train. Mr. Ivey was bloody around the face, and his clothes looked as if they had been slept in. And the neighbour didn't look wealthy.

The young girl at the reception desk said, "It will cost a good deal of money to have a room in the hospital. Do you think you can afford it?"

The neighbour, barely able to restrain his amusement, answered, "The two of us together can surely take care of the money. This just happens to be J. B. Ivey, one of the wealthy chain-store owners in the South. He may look like a tramp in his gardening outfit but I think he could buy this hospital without impairing his bank account."

The neighbour himself told me this when I was spending a week at beautiful Lake Junaluska. Of course, I had to visit Mr. Ivey's colorful dahlia gardens, which overlook the blue lake fringed by mountains. There I found that the fascinating thing about this ageless, eighty-year-old Methodist layman, who owns large stores in Charlotte, Greenville, Asheville, Orlando, and Daytona Beach, is not the fact that he looks like Emerson nor that he still holds a firm hand on his department stores, but his collection of hobbies. Among all these the dahlia garden comes first. Not only does he have dahlias by the thousands, but his garden contains some of the most beautiful dahlias in the country.

Mr. Ivey is also interested in tulips. Each spring at tulip time he has a tulip fair in his gardens at Charlotte, and tens of thousands of people come from all over the Southland to see his marvellous displays.

In front of his garden near Lake Junaluska he sets out vases of cut flowers each morning, and the sign says, "Take one." By noon not one flower is left, and many passers-by have had their lives brightened by this method of sharing beauty.

Of course, Junaluska itself is one of Mr. Ivey's hobbies. He is one of the founders and builders. Here on these beautiful shores, in a home overlooking the lake nestling in the mist-shrouded Smokies, within sight of its fifteen-foot lighted cross, this man, who might go to any spot in the world, chooses to spend his summers. He attends the services in the tabernacle, sitting in the front row, and usually at night wearing a little black skull cap which, incidentally, a Jewish rabbi friend in Charlotte gave him.

Another hobby of his is children. He loves them, and they love him. He financed and still supports a beautifully equipped playground on the lake shore. Every morning when he is at the lake he spends some time playing with the children. He amuses them with sleight-of-hand tricks and magical arts, which he studies carefully.

His real hobby hasn't been mentioned—it is just being a good Christian layman and churchman. He is a loyal member and Sunday-school teacher at First Church, Charlotte, where he is usually in his place at worship services, prayer meetings, official board sessions, and Sunday school.

His interest in the church goes back beyond that evening when, a lad of eleven, he attended a camp meeting with his preacher-father. "I found God at that meeting," he says, "and one of the preachers took me aside and told me he was glad to see me take that stand for God.

"It has always been my policy to change my church work every four or five years," he added. "I suppose I got this from my father, who, as a preacher, was changed in his pastorate every four years.

"But in spite of the fact that I often change my church work from teaching a Sunday-school class to ushering, to service on the Board of Stewards, or, even to janitoring on a limited scale, I am always working in and for the church in some form, and I do it because I love the church."

For several summers it has been my pleasure to meet this layman at Junaluska, where he is a never-failing front-row auditor, not only to my particular addresses, but to all the speakers who go to that great institution. His very presence each summer on those grounds, his constant attendance at the services, his personally directed programs for the children each morning, daily gifts of dahlias in front of his home, and his daily decorations of the platform of the auditorium with his personally raised flowers is a form of simple, everyday service which is an inspiration to all who visit those beautiful grounds.

XV

"THIS MAN SOWED FAITH"

"This man sowed faith wherever he moved.
It was in hand when he held yours at meeting.
Never so called out of yourself, never so loved
Were you or anyone as by this in greeting."

THE POETESS, May Sarton of Cambridge, Massachusetts, was writing about Dr. Cabot, the author of *What Men Live By*. She entitled her poem, *The White-Haired Man*, and I was much impressed by it.

When I read it for the first time I thought how well it fitted another personality whom I had interviewed, Judge Edgar Vaught of Oklahoma City, of whom I had heard for many years from his many friends. During my conversations with the late Carl McGee, brother of Bishop McGee of Chicago, inventor of the parking meter and the man who unearthed and brought to light the scandal of Tea Pot Dome, I had heard Judge Vaught's name mentioned frequently.

Other men who knew Judge Vaught well were Clay Doss, first vice-president of the Nash Motor Company, and Fred Jones, head of all Ford business in the state of Oklahoma, one of the richest and most useful citizens in the state.

All three of these men were started on the road to fame and fortune by Judge Vaught, who, for more than thirty-five years taught a large Sunday-school class in Oklahoma City. These men were boys in his class.

Judge Vaught derives great and genuine satisfaction from teaching his Sunday-school class, but the public knows him for something else: he has been much in the news as a judge in a Federal court. He conducted the trial of the kidnappers of Charles F. Urschel, an Oklahoma City oil millionaire, and sent four of the kidnappers to the penitentiary. George (Machine-Gun) Kelley and his red-haired wife, Katherine; Boss Shannon, and Albert Bates—as desperate a gang of criminals as this country has ever known, are all serving time in Alcatraz, for no mercy was shown them. They were cruel and desperate brigands.

Judge Vaught does not relish this so-called fame, but it will cling to him as long as he lives because of the human drama connected with it.

Appointed to the Federal judgeship by President Coolidge in 1928, he came to this high place just in time to join in the battle against the many kidnapping cases which began with that of the Lindbergh baby's kidnapping and death and came to a climax in the Urschel case.

When I interviewed the judge, a genial, friendly, grey-haired, rather rotund person, the very first thing he said was, "Reporters and interviewers always want me to talk about the Urschel case, but that is now past history, and any Federal judge would have done exactly what I did. That case just happened to throw me into the newspaper spotlight. I'm much prouder of my church connections and my Sunday-school class than I am of that spectacular kidnapping case. Let's talk about that."

I agreed, for I was interested in the fact that for fifty years he had been a faithful, loyal layman in the Methodist

Church, and all of those years he has been teaching Sunday school—and was proud of it.

Thirty-six of those years he has served as teacher of an adult Bible Class at St. Luke's Methodist Church in Oklahoma City. Over that period the class has ranged from one hundred to five hundred in attendance, with an average of two hundred and fifty.

"How have you kept the class members coming all through those years?" I asked him, because I happened to know that those members had the habit of starting in the judge's class when they were young men and following through with him during their early married lives, and into mature years when their families had become larger. One man in the city told me that half of the children in those families called the Judge "Pop."

His reply was, "I teach them the Bible, and that never grows stale or old. It is always new and it is always news. Then we discuss a little philosophy, a little law, and a lot of humanity, which includes, love, romance, home, children, and religion. Those are always new themes, no matter how often we discuss them. The Bible stories are old ones, but the class can always find some new angle for discussion. I have never found any more fascinating stories than the Bible stories. In fact, I never tell them a new story."

After he had taught this same class for twenty-five years, the class had a great celebration and presented him with a plaque of recognition, which I found hanging on the wall of his office, the proudest decoration he has in his office, and to which he points with more pride than to any of the innumerable honors, tributes, and recognitions he has received as a Federal judge and as one of the pioneers of not only Oklahoma City but of the whole state of Oklahoma. He has been associated with Sunday-school work, either as a superintendent or as a teacher for more than fifty years.

It had been suggested that I talk with the city's most prominent business man, Fred Jones, and find out from him about this nationally-known Methodist layman. Besides being the Ford representative, Mr. Jones is an owner of radio stations, oil fields, hotels, and newspapers, and a wealthy man. I had been told that "Fred is one of Judge Vaught's boys."

This is Fred's story, as told by himself: "I came to Oklahoma City as a poor boy peddling kitchen utensils from house to house, homeless and lonely. I was invited to Judge Vaught's Sunday-school class, and there I found friends, ideals, learning, and a place in this community. All I know of goodness, friendship, character, and good citizenship I learned from that class."

Later Mr. Jones rummaged through his files, pulled out a frayed, yellow clipping from the *Oklahoma News,* and said, "This is the type of fearless, pioneering person the judge is. Read it, doctor!" This is part of what I read:

"We have remarked previously in these columns concerning the wise and precedent-shattering attitude of Judge Vaught on crime publicity as evidenced during the course of the Urschel kidnaping trial. Read this frank statement of the veteran Federal judge:

" 'At the suggestion of the Attorney-General of this nation, and with apologies to no one, this court here has permitted facilities for the widest publicity in this case, with the hope that it will have a tendency to deter crime in the future.

" 'The pitiless light of publicity will do more to unpopularize crime and arouse the public to stamp it out than any other single factor.

" 'We are living in an age of pictures when people get their information from seeing as well as reading. The pictures of criminals, chained and before the bar of justice, will do much to stamp out kidnaping.

" 'The courts belong to the people. Only a few people can get inside the courtroom, and the Constitution says that our trials shall be open and above board for all.

" 'Those who can't get into this courtroom should know what is going on through the newspapers. America wants no secret trials, no secret prosecution of accused persons.'

"Thus, this kindly, Sunday-school-teaching Federal judge, who carried out his announced intention to 'put teeth into this kidnap law,' was pioneering a new field in publicity just as much as he was making history in American jurisprudence with his sweeping interpretation of the law inspired by the kidnaping and murder of the Charles A. Lindbergh baby."

This is the comment of a great city newspaper, the *Oklahoma News*. And that is exactly what this kindly layman did do. He gave pitiless publicity to one of the greatest kidnapping trials in American history, and put "teeth" into the Lindbergh law—so much so that there has not been another kidnapping in Oklahoma since that trial. Thus a layman has pioneered in a new field of publicity and given the nation a greater sense of security.

Carl McGee, himself one of the most noted characters in the great Southwest, a famous editor also, said to me, "Judge Vaught is one of the finest Christian gentlemen I have ever known, and he would be news to any newspaper or magazine in this nation. I owe much to his support in my trying days."

Clay Doss, now vice-president of Nash-Kelvinator and

one of the nation's greatest automobile executives, said,
"When I went to Oklahoma City as a young college graduate I was invited to Judge Vaught's Sunday-school class,
and that was the greatest single influence for good that
ever came into my life. I could never repay that great man
for the good he did for me."

Fred Jones commented, "Judge Vaught, in his Sunday-
school class, did more for the Christian thinking and living of this section than any living man, and I owe everything I have and am to his fine Christian influence."

This is a living dramatization of Christian service
through personality, which inspires us all to carry on in
this spirit, the spirt of Judge Vaught and of innumerable
men like him, and in the spirit of May Sarton's poem, the
first verse of which I quoted at the beginning of this chapter and the last verses of which I quote to end this chapter:

"For he kept nothing of the thirsting flood;
   It poured through him, unstinted, like a river;
   A quickening essence, transfused through the blood.
   Afterwards strength was in you, he the giver.
   For this man each was given holiness in trust;
   Each with a secret gift, and none the same,
   The gift of healing, healing because you must;
   Because healing was in you in God's name.
   Never doubt; never find it out too late,
   But, now, flower and bear fruit in human meeting;
   Love, not transcending the person, but incarnate,
   As in his own hand given you in greeting."

XVI

"WHEN THE HIGH HEART WE MAGNIFY"

FOR MANY YEARS I have been specialising in interviewing famous men and women. It has been a thrilling experience. I have put the material into a national broadcast under the title, "Great American Personalities."

While carrying out these journalistic chores, I have been guided by a little quatrain from John Drinkwater, who said in his drama, *Abraham Lincoln*:

> "When the high heart we magnify,
> And the sure vision celebrate,
> And worship greatness passing by,
> Ourselves are great."

Side by side with that English poet's observation, I have always placed an immortal Tennysonian definition of true greatness, which runs:

> "In me there dwells
> No greatness, save it be some far-off touch
> Of greatness to know well I am not great!"

Therefore, it is of another group that I wish to write now—the near-great, the humble great, the great who do not know that they are great, the heroic, humble people who have lived like Christ and whose names have never got into any *Who's Who*.

One of those great souls happens to be a Negro whom I

have known for thirty years. He is a janitor by occupation. His name is Saunders Wilkins. He was the janitor in the Boston University School of Theology for more than thirty years. I knew him first when I was a student in that school back in 1909 and 1910. Now that I have been a teacher in that same school for fifteen years, I feel that I am able to judge this man fairly.

First of all, Saunders Wilkins never had any education himself, and he has always worked with his hands and muscles, although he is intuitively and mentally a smart man. His usual hours, both in winter and summer, were from four o'clock in the morning to ten o'clock at night; and he is still, in spite of retirement, on that same schedule, because he wants to be.

Second, Wilkins has raised a family, and one of his sons, a college graduate, has attained a high place in the ranks of science, and in the service of his nation he wore the insignia of a captain. Another of his sons graduated from college, came to the same school where his father was janitor, and was graduated with honours. He is now the pastor of an important church in Nashville, and is honoured and respected. And my guess is that this father has never in all his labouring life had a wage that was more than one hundred twenty-five dollars a month. Yet he has managed to do all of this and see two sons through college and into positions of trust and service in the life of the Church and the nation. And I call that true greatness in the best sense of that word.

Third, this humble man is one of the finest Christian gentlemen I have ever known—bar none. And though there are twenty professors in this school of theology—most of whom are or have been preachers and are expected both

to teach and to live the highest type of a Christian life—I
do not believe that there is one of us who would not be fair
enough to say of this janitor, in the immortal words of
Kipling, "You're a better man than I am, Gunga Din!"

And if by chance there might be a single professor
among all of those ministers who would hesitate to give a
high place among the saints to this janitor, of one thing I
am certain—there are no students who would deny him the
honour. What I am trying to say is that a Negro janitor
in a Methodist theological school outranks us all as a
Christian. Sickness, suffering, defeat, financial struggle,
disaster, disappointment, and unkind and unjust treatment have been his lot through a long life of friendliness
and good will. And yet I have never known him to speak
unkindly of a student or of any person who did him ill.
He has been the perfect example of a man who knew how
to forgive, and did forgive, those who treated him unkindly, and he has heaped more coals of fire on more bald
and haughty heads than any single person I have known
in my lifetime. I have yet to see my friend in a vindictive
spirit or seeking revenge for any evil that has been done
him. He is always smiling, always friendly, and always has
a sense of humour.

During these thirty years Saunders, our friend and janitor, has worn the cast-off clothing of professors, preachers,
and bishops; but he makes no apology for that, because he
has done it through sheer necessity—the necessity of getting his children enough to eat, providing them their
early education, and finally putting them through college
and into positions of responsibility. In fact, he wears those
cast-off clothes with rare dignity and good humour. He
honours the clothes he wears, and he is grateful for them.

Also, during these thirty years, Saunders has seen literally thousands of students graduate from the halls of the Boston University School of Theology, many of them to become college presidents, bishops, and pastors. The friendship he won while they were students because he was always the Christian gentleman he has maintained ever since.

These leaders honour him today. And when I go out to speak in their churches, the first man they ask about is not the dean of the school, the president of the university, or any of the professors. Instead, they first say, "How is good old Saunders?" When they come back to the old halls for a visit, the first person they want to see is the janitor, and they make their way down four flights of stairs into the dark recesses of the boiler room for a friendly reunion.

Saunders Wilkins has won an immortal place in the hearts of the graduates of Boston University School of Theology because he has literally lived all these thirty years by the spirit of the text, "The Son of man came not to be ministered unto, but to minister, and to give his life a ransom for many." Saunders has certainly lived heroically for Christ.

XVII

"A MAN WHO GOT A GLORY"

It is no small matter of news that the outstanding man in professional baseball is a Protestant layman who is proud of his church, his religion, and his business. That man is Branch Rickey, currently president of the Brooklyn Dodgers club, but for many years associated with the Saint Louis Cardinals, who won the World Series five times under his leadership.

Now, Branch Rickey is the type of a man who does not hide his religious and denominational interests under a bushel. He makes no apologies to anybody for the time he spends at church work. In fact, he is proud of his church interests and fills a speaking engagement at a General Conference, a young people's rally, a Methodist Crusade, or a local church meeting with pride and power. He always reminds me of a quatrain by Berton Braley, for many years his personal friend, who once sang:

> "The battle might be gory
> And the odds unfair,
> But the men who got a glory
> Never knew despair."

One of the first stories that Branch Rickey ever told me when he was my football coach back in 1906 at Allegheny College concerned his father. On a farm near Lucasville, Ohio, the elder Rickey used to take his sons out to the field where they had a pet bull. The boys would grab the bull's tail and see who could hold on the longest.

Of course, the bull naturally resented the violation of his personal dignity and infringement on his natural right to be let alone so long as he behaved himself. He would start, pell-mell, across the pasture, trying to shake off the boy hanging on, and bellow, jump, twist, and turn. The boy who held on the longest won the game. Since that long-ago day Branch Rickey has had hold of a good many hard problems, but he has managed to hold on until he won.

Born in Lucasville, Branch Rickey grew up in a good old-fashioned Methodist home, went to Ohio Wesleyan in 1900, played professional ball even while he was in college, coached football at Ohio Wesleyan and at Allegheny College, both church institutions. In 1905 he went to law school at the University of Michigan and coached the university baseball team to pay his tuition. During his summer vacations while at law school, he played with the Cincinnati Reds, but he was fired because he refused to play Sunday ball. One day he told me the reason: "Before I left Lucasville I promised my mother that I would never play Sunday ball."

In those days they called Rickey "The Deacon," "Sissy," or "The Sunday-school Catcher." He was hooted, sneered at, derided; and yet for thirty years he has stuck to his principles of fighting booze and gambling and refusing to attend Sunday baseball.

One day I asked Rick about that promise to his mother, for, after all, his teams do play Sunday games. This is what he said to me: "When I first went to Houston to play professional ball my mother called me into the front room and said to me: 'Now, remember your home training and church, Branch, and don't play Sunday ball—for my sake.'"

"I promised mother I wouldn't, and I have kept my promise. My mother meant everything to me and I wouldn't go back on a promise to her if the heavens fell down. I'm no prude, and I know that it seems inconsistent when professional baseball is actually played on Sunday to say that I won't play or attend games; but I intend to keep my promise to my mother, and that's that!"

Branch Rickey not only grew up in a Methodist home and graduated from a Methodist college, but for many years he has been a faithful trustee of Ohio Wesleyan University, and his intimate friends are Methodist bishops, preachers, and laymen all over this land. He is a loyal member of the Methodist Church in St. Louis and has always attended church regularly and taken an active part in official board metings. He has long taught a Sunday-school class. He takes an energetic part in both local and national church affairs.

When he was in college he was captain of the football team while Homer Rodeheaver was cheer leader, and they have always remained fast friends. One day I asked Rickey what religion meant to him and this is what he said: "It means everything. From boyhood on I have had a growing religious experience. I want to live the ideals of Christ every day of my life, in business and on the athletic field. I want my responses to every situation to rise as automatically Christian as my nervous responses in driving an automobile are." And he means just that.

Few people know that Rickey's life has not all been easy sailing. He graduated from law school and settled in

Boise, Idaho, in 1907. His law office was in the same building with Senator William E. Borah, who lent him law books, because the young lawyer could not afford to buy his own. When Borah campaigned the first time for senator, Branch Rickey went out on the stump for him and, is credited with having had a large part in the election.

During those Idaho years he got an infection in his hand and nearly died. There was little income from law and he had to go back to the St. Louis Browns as a baseball scout to make a living. He had started out in his law practice with three college friends, with whom he lived in a sort of a co-operative arrangement. They shared the same house. When Branch went back to baseball, he agreed that he would divide his salary with his two friends until they got on their feet. Of course, he kept his promise, always expecting to go back to law after a few years. But opportunities in baseball opened such a large field of influence that he stayed in it.

In 1909 he developed such a serious throat infection that he had to go to Saranac Lake for three months. He wasn't sure whether he would ever get out of that sanitarium, but his old determination to hold on to life, learned partly through that boyhood game of holding on to the bull's tail, came to his rescue, and after three months he was back as manager of the Browns.

From that time on his baseball career is well known to most readers. From the Browns he went to the Cardinals, who did not even have money enough to buy uniforms or to engage in spring practice. He made them one of the richest and most successful teams in the nation before going to the Brooklyn Dodgers.

Everybody knows that Branch Rickey organized what

was called "The Knot-Hole Gang," to let boys into the games free if they were vouched for by preachers, social workers, or the Y.M.C.A. He also originated the "farm system" now used by many clubs and, as one sports writer says, "gave baseball a college education."

"The Knot-Hole Gang" was an expression of Branch Rickey's sense of social responsibility and a means of serving young boys by keeping them from the streets, gang temptations, and pool rooms. The only requirement that a "Knot-Hole-Gang boy" had to meet to get a free ticket to a ball game was to have a Y.M.C.A. Secretary, a preacher, or a social worker vouch for him. That was his ticket of admission to a national league game. The movement started in St. Louis and spread all over the country. One social worker in New York City, Mr. Albert Hines, head of the Madison Square Boys Club, whom Branch Rickey once coached in football at Allegheny College, once said to me: "Rickey's 'Knot-Hole Gang' idea has done more to solve the juvenile delinquency problem than any other single factor in American life."

The "farm club" idea was organized for two purposes: first, to bring a steady supply of new ball players into the big leagues from high schools and junior colleges, second, to give unknown boys a chance at big league baseball. Rickey has always looked upon himself as a father to these young and promising boys and has always held up high standards of morality and social responsibility to them. They all call him "Mr. Rickey," and go to him with their personal, domestic and financial problems. It is the family spirit in professional baseball.

But perhaps the greatest expression of Christian service which Branch Rickey has pioneered is illustrated in Jackie

Robinson's story. Here was the first Negro boy who ever attained to a permanent opportunity in baseball. The racial prejudice in America had always kept Negro boys from their chance at big league ball. But Branch Rickey deliberately paved and pioneered the way for this breakdown of racial prejudice in professional baseball as the ultimate expression of his sense of Christian service and social responsibility.

Few people know that in World War I Branch Rickey went to France and became a major before the war was over, then came back to organise a syndicate which purchased the defunct Cardinals.

Back in the Lucasville days Branch met and married Jane Moulton at church. They have six children.

Several years ago I was in their home, sitting beside a huge wood fire. It was Sunday evening and Mrs. Rickey was hurrying the children off to Epworth League. It was as natural for those husky children to be hurrying off to League as for the children of any minister's home.

Branch Rickey has gone to the top in professional baseball, but he has also gone to the top in his church, for he has spoken in every type of institution that his church knows, from official board to General Conference. In fact, the church world is still talking about a great address on Christian living which he made at a General Conference.

There is a glory about Branch Rickey's career in baseball, and, if I am any judge of men, that glory came because he had a Christian experience about which he is willing to testify, both inside and outside of baseball circles. That glory came into his life because he has his greatest satisfactions in his home and in his church. His life is a true reflection of Christian service.

XVIII

FAITHFUL FOR FIFTY YEARS

WHENEVER MY READER sees or rides in one of those silvery, sleek, streamlined trains with the reclining seats, or on a swift, graceful plane, he is probably getting acquainted with a product made by the late Edward G. Budd, a Christian layman of Philadelphia, Pennsylvania. And since Mr. Budd was president of the Budd Wheel Company, as well as of the Edward G. Budd Manufacturing Company, the traveller on a train or bus to almost any place in the country will probably find that the wheels he hears purring along the highway, or singing as they click over the steel rail connections, were made by Mr. Budd and his associates. This layman probably has done more than any other single manufacturer to put the nation on wheels.

My first knowledge of Mr. Budd and all his works came in the early twenties, when I was interviewing William Stout, the foremost designer and engineer of streamlined trains, automobiles, and airplanes in America, and, incidentally, the son of a Methodist minister. He had just designed a pioneer streamliner, made for the run from Chicago across mountain and desert to California. Mr. Stout suggested that if I wanted to write about a real man, I should not bother with him or with any of the prominent auto manufacturers. "Go get an interview with Mr. Budd," he said. "He's the real manufacturing genius of to-day, and I just work for him. I did the Union Pacific train for his company. In addition to that, since you are a preacher, and I am a preacher's son, you will be interested in knowing that he is one of the finest Christian churchmen I ever knew. He is also a Christian gentleman in his business relations. I have never worked with a finer man in my life."

The next day I happened to be talking with Henry Ford. I asked him about Mr. Budd, and this is what he said; "He is a high-class Christian gentleman, just the type of a man I like to see in the manufacturing world. They are far too few to suit me."

Years later I encountered a young fellow named Henry Budd in one of my homiletics classes at Boston University School of Theology. He married Phyllis Leonard, daughter of Bishop Adna Leonard, and I watched them go out into the ministry, establish a home, and become successful in the ministry. Young Henry Budd is now pastor of University Church, Ithaca, New York.

It was two years before I found out that this promising young student was a nephew of Edward G. Budd. Soon after making this discovery I remarked to Henry: "It's rather interesting that you are a minister and come from one of America's great industrial families."

"Nothing unusual if you know our family," was his answer. We have always been strong churchmen, and my uncle is as much, if not more, interested in church work, than he is in his manufacturing business. He is every bit as much a churchman as he is an industrialist. Back in 1796 his great-grandfather, Dr. William Budd was one of the original founders and trustees of the First Methodist Church in Germantown, Pa., which observed its 150th anniversary last June. There has been a Budd on the official board or board of trustees all through these years. Yes, we're Methodists from away back!"

The Budd family has many church connections. At Dover, Delaware, I learned that a brother of Mr. Budd had been the pioneering president of the Wesley Junior college there. During the week of services there appeared the mother of young Henry Budd, who is the sister of the well-known industrialist. Here I was getting all tangled up with a famous family which has been all tangled up with the church work for years. Through those years they have worked simply, quietly, unostentatiously as laymen, as well as preachers and college presidents. They seem to have been born for the purpose.

But that was not all of it. Before the summer was over, I had another association with the Budds at Ocean City, a summer camp meeting spot on the Jersey shore not far from Philadelphia. A grey-haired man and his wife came up after the sermon. The manager of the grounds seemed a bit excited about the man and whispered his name, but I did not catch it. Then he said, "I want you to meet Mr. Edward Budd and his wife."

I knew why he had become excited, and so was I. Here, on a hot July Sunday evening, at an old-fashioned camp meeting service, was one of the nation's most distinguished manufacturers.

I expressed my surprise to the manager, and this was his reply; "This is just where Mr. Budd would most want to be. In fact, he attends these camp meeting services regularly."

As I thought more about it I realised that this was exactly what we should expect of a man with a century and a half of church ancestry.

I wanted to know something about the everyday church relationships of this distinguished layman, and I asked the man who could tell me, the pastor of his church.

"Mr. Budd has been a member of our church for fifty years," said Rev. Paul W. Hoon. "He and Mrs. Budd came into the church by transfer on October 5, 1899."

"That's a long membership," I said.

"And, more than that, the records show that they have occupied the same pew in the church all of these fifty years. And even more than that, he is always in his pew on Sunday when he is in town. Mr. and Mrs. Budd naturally travel widely, but when they are at home I can always be sure that they will be sitting in that same family pew, attentively listening to my sermon, good or bad, and taking a reverent and definite part in the worship."

"What part does Mr. Budd take in the actual church work?" I asked the pastor.

"Through all the fifty years of his membership here in First Church he has had an active part in all our work and has given us the advantage of his business experience. Back in 1920 he organized the first Every Member Canvass in this church. He has been a member of our official board and a steward for most of the years of his membership. At present he is vice-president of the Board of Trustees. His wife has been prominently active in our Woman's Society of Christian Service for many years, and her special philanthropic interest is the Methodist Home for Orphans here in Philadelphia, in which she is an officer and a director.

"Mr. Budd's work takes him away a great deal, but if he is anywhere near Philadelphia, he is in church Sunday morning. He takes his religious duties as faithfully as any person in my congregation. He attends our dinners and many of our fellowship meetings for prayer. He takes a special interest in young men. He is an intensely devout man, a man of prayer, of Christian integrity, and, all in all, one of the best products of Methodism at its best."

XIX

HE PRAYED FOR HIS PREACHER

HERE IS A story of Christian service which has run through three generations, first, through "Grandfather Crummey," the founder of the Bean Spray Pump Company in San José, California, who gave most of what he made to missions and the church all his life. I was his pastor for three years and could always count on him for special help in any project I wanted to undertake, because he always tithed and he always had plenty of money in what he called "The Lord's Fund."

Not only did he tithe, but Grandfather Crummey was always in his pew for both morning and evening church services. He always sat on the front seat at both prayer meeting and class meeting, always taught a Sunday-school Class, and never missed an official Board meeting. If ever the phrase "a pillar of the church" applied to a man it was to that stalwart man.

And now there is a member of the third generation of the Crummey family who is serving the church—Clifford Crummey, a young minister in California, who also served his valiant day as a chaplain in the recent war. I baptised this boy in the First Church, San José, when he was a baby, and both his father and grandfather were present. I well remember that the old gentleman remarked to me, rather wistfully and facetiously, and with a broad grin, "You may have baptised the first preacher in the Crummey family this morning." I smiled and replied, "It could be!"

And that is exactly what happened, for twenty years later that same boy whom I had baptised as a baby, the third member of the Crummey clan to serve the church, walked into our Boston University School of Theology, and said to me, with a big, wide grin, "Lafayette, here I come!"

I watched this boy solicitiously through his seminary years, saw him meet his wife as he served a small student church in Providence, Rhode Island; watched him graduate, and saw him go out into the chaplaincy and ultimately into the ministry in California, a glorious climax to three generations who had served the church. And as I watched him go into the ministry two devoted lay ancestors smiled down on him and on me, for I saw in that boy of the third generation the fruition of three generations of Christian service. And now back one generation to the story of his father, John Crummey, president of Food Machinery, one of the nation-wide industrial organizations which did valiant service during the war years:

Every time you saw one of those "water buffaloes"—amphibian landing craft—going ashore on some Pacific island you were looking at a product of the Food Machinery Company, of which John Crummey, a Christian layman, was president.

Now, John Crummey had half a dozen sons, grandsons, and sons-in-law in the armed services scattered around the world, from the South Seas to Europe. Several of them actually rode ashore in the craft produced by the Food Machinery Company.

One of the sons, Clifford Crummey, was a chaplain for two years. I watched him as he went through the College of the Pacific at Stockton, editing his college paper and making a notable record. Finally, as I have said I had him in my classes in Boston University School of Theology. John Crummey was more proud of the fact that Clifford was a Navy chaplain than he was of the fact that his company was building the all-important landing craft for water-to-land operations.

Food Machinery owns the patents which color citrus fruit. There was a long struggle over those patents in the courts, but now Food Machinery controls them.

The founder of these interests used to tithe his income at San José. He was the largest contributor to missions that I have ever known. During World War I he sent me a large check to St. Nazaire, France, to have Biblical quotations printed on attractive circulars and distributed to the soldiers.

John Crummey has carried on the tithing traditions of his generous father and is one of the most liberal supporters of missions and home church projects.

He is generous not only with his money, but also with his time and talent, too. He is faithful in his church attendance and in his duties as a teacher of a young men's class in First Church, San José. I have heard him say more than once in Boston, "I'll have to take a plane so I can get back to my Sunday-school class Sunday morning."

When his son Clifford was in the seminary we both tried to persuade John Crummey to stay over in Boston for Sunday, but he could not be convinced. "I've got to get back to my boys," he said, and get back he did. We took him down to the Boston airport and he boarded a plane that put him into San José in time to teach his class. And my guess is that John Crummey does as much thinking, planning, and studying for that class as he spends for running Food Machinery.

Naturally, his income is none of my business, but I know it is large. But you would not suspect that he is a rich man by the way he lives. The only mark of wealth he shows is that he has a swimming pool at his commodious home. And that pool practically belongs to the church and the town, so generously is it shared. Young people of churches of all denominations use it. Young people from the underprivileged areas enjoy its cool waters. They use it as though it were their own private club.

If I were to make a good guess about the one thing from which Mr. Crummey gets the deepest satisfaction, it would be that his son is a minister. I suspect that John himself always had an inner hunger to be a preacher. He is an excellent speaker—alive, alert, ready of speech. He frequently addresses church gatherings and holds his audience tense with what I like to call "the eloquence of facts."

He has been a valuable member of the Book Committee and now the Board of Publication of the Methodist Church. He gives of his business advice and experience to all Methodist projects on the Pacific Coast. He has been a member of a number of General Conferences and an intimate friend of dozens of bishops, editors, and church leaders.

Methodism on the Pacific Coast counts on John Crummey's tithe for many of its religious, social, and educational projects. In fact, he supports Methodist institutions around the world. (Incidentally, he helped us at Boston start the first radio course in a theological seminary.) He does not let his left hand know what his right hand does in the disposals of his tithe, but many a preacher could tell you if John would allow it.

But the best support he gives the church is spiritual rather than financial. Here is an illustration:

When I went to First Church, San José, I was nervous over my first morning in that great pulpit. I went to it in fear and trembling. But when I walked into my study for a few moments of quiet, the janitor of the church, a retired minister, said to me: "Mr. Crummey was in this study this morning. I came in to brush up and found him on his knees beside your chair, praying. I apologized for my intrusion and he said to me: 'I was just offering a little prayer for our new preacher. I asked God to bless him as he sits in this chair preparing his sermons for us.'"

I confess to weeping a little at that good news. John Crummey and I had been fellow workers at an Epworth League Institute at Asilomar. When I went into the pulpit I was on fire with the thought that I had come to serve a church which had a layman who could and would do a gracious, kindly, loving, spiritual thing like that. And it is probable that I would never have heard of it if the janitor had not talked with me that morning.

A church is very fortunate when it has men who are enough concerned about its welfare not only to tithe and teach a class through a quarter of a century, but also to get down on their knees at the study chair of their minister and pray God's blessings on his efforts.

XX

"HOW DO THEY DO IT?"

SEVERAL YEARS AGO, an alert, far-sighted, and yet contemporary editor of a great church magazine, *The Christian Herald*, Dr. Frank S. Mead, who now, incidentally, is editorial adviser of the company which is publishing this book, sent me on an assignment to discover how it was and is that ministers on such low salaries seem to be able to maintain a high standard of living, purchase books and clothes, and send their children to college. As we talked about the assignment, he said, "How do they do it?"

"That's the perfect title for this piece," I replied.

"So let it be," he remaked laconically, turning his mind to other pressing matters.

Thus it was that I was sent out on the interesting research which produced at least the content if not the form of this chapter on stewardship and tithing in the lives of preachers, without which this book would not be complete.

In that motion picture story of a preacher's life, "One Foot in Heaven," the wife is in a store purchasing some food. When the storekeeper told her the price, she, who always travelled on a low margin and had to count the cost of every item, had a look of dismay on her face, for it was during World War I, and prices were going up every day. The storekeeper, seeing her dismayed look, said to her, "I know things are going up but wages have increased too."

144

The preacher's wife replied, with a question in her tone, "I suppose they have."

That dialogue tells the whole story I want to tell in this chapter. Those of us who know the small incomes which ministers receive, and what miracles they and their wives and families work with those small incomes, are constantly saying to ourselves, "How *do* they do it?"

The very intonation of Mrs. Spence's answer to the storekeeper's statement that wages were going up, "I suppose they have," really said, "Wages may have gone up but we preachers' families haven't discovered it yet."

It is a striking coincidence, perhaps, but, nevertheless, a noticeable one, that in recent years the church press has been paying a good deal of attention to the economic problem confronting ministers. In *Zions Herald* appeared an article entitled "The High Cost of Low Salaries," in which A. Ritchie Low showed how low salaries undermine ministers' morale and their ability to do their best work. *The Christian Advocate* published another article, entitled "He Wouldn't Pay His Bills." It was written by an anonymous preacher about his own experience—a pathetic, tragic, and awakening article. I wrote an article for the *Ladies Home Journal* entitled "The Church Just Doesn't Think."

When a secular magazine like the *Ladies Home Journal* concerns itself with the plight of the minister on a low salary it is time that we of the church concern ourselves about it also. But this chapter is not the start of a crusade for higher salaries for ministers. Its purpose is to state and answer the question it puts, "How Do They Do It?" meaning how do ministers manage to raise large families, send them through college, keep up the personal appearance they have to keep, be in the public eye, entertain every group in the church in their homes at their own expense, get a college and a theological education of seven years' duration, as they are now expected to do, own and operate an automobile, buy the latest books, belong to noonday lunch clubs and lodges, and pay their share to every public appeal that comes along, which they are expected to do and to do generously? How *do* they do it?

When I wrote this chapter I immediately thought of old Father Hughes, six feet tall, a giant in stature as well as in the ministry. When I was a boy in West Virginia his name was magic, for he was the greatest preacher of his generation. I knew that during his ministry his top salary was $1400. I knew that he had raised a family of seven children. I knew that he sent five of his children to college and that three of them had received their degrees. I knew that at one time he had three of his sons in West Virginia University at the same time, and that at that time his salary was only $1200. I also knew that two of those sons graduated and became bishops, Matthew Simpson Hughes and Edwin Holt Hughes. That seemed to me to be the classic illustration of how a preacher and his wife can do so much on so little. Therefore I wrote to my friend, Bishop Edwin Holt Hughes, in Washington, and asked him to tell me how his father did it.

Bishop Hughes answered immediately, saying:

"My father's upper limit of salary was $1400, and he always tithed that, and his house. Most of the time it was $1200 or under. At one time when we children were young it was only $800. Of course, that was more than it would be now when you think of the additional demands that are made on a contemporary minister and the higher cost of living. Also, in my father's day it was the common practice in small towns and country pulpits for the members to make frequent donations of food and clothing. Whenever a parishioner killed a hog the parsonage received generous portions of that 'butchering.' In the fall, when harvest was at its height, the preacher's bins, cellar and storerooms were filled to overflowing with winter food. Whenever a neighbour woman baked bread, pies or other dainties, they always shared with the preacher and his family. That was the custom. It is not so now. What we called 'Missionary Barrels' were often shared, not only with missionaries in foreign lands but they were also sent to rural and Home Mission and small town ministers; and a surprising lot of wearable clothes were always found in the 'Barrel.' We have none of that in the modern church. Farmers shared their milk, butter, eggs, and fruit with their ministers in the old days, but that habit is no longer in vogue. Therefore, I say that my father's $1400 salary with those additional perquisites would be a much smaller salary in these days.

" 'How did he do it?' Well, my father was not at all a businessman; but he had a horror of debt, and he was economical to the extreme. But mother was the main secret. She was the answer to the question, 'How Do They Do It?' She was a good 'businessman.' She saved and scrimped and got ready for the 'rainy day.' That 'rainy day' was always a part of her prophecy and of her expectations. When the time came for me to go to Ohio Wesleyan University and father was in financial despair, she would appear with a long black stocking (literally a stocking—I can see it yet) and play the provident banker by handing over twenty-five to fifty dollars, a portion of her tithe. In addition to that, the boys all worked, as preachers' sons I know have worked and do work, and made some money. From eighteen onward I cared for myself entirely, selling photographs, soliciting advertisements and winning some prize money. And I guess I didn't have a hard time either, yet I was no plutocrat. It was mainly because my dear old mother did her own washing, made the clothes of all of her six children, cooked for us, and acted as banker for the whole family. The secret of raising our large family of seven and sending five of them to college lay largely with my mother and the fact that we had a co-operative spirit in the family, and that the family income was always tithed. What belonged to one belonged to all. All of us were gloriously happy in our work."

"How do they do it?" Well, I have an answer out of my own experience. In my first church in San Francisco, to which I was appointed by that same Bishop Hughes whose story has just been told, we got just eighty dollars a month. We had a baby, and we had to pay twenty dollars a month rent. We had a hard time making both ends meet, but we did it. I remember that on Monday evening we usually made our dinner out of a ham bone that Mr. Mobbs, our loyal grocer, had given us when he closed his store at the week-end. So we had that ham bone straight, or we made it into soup with beans. On Tuesday I got ten cents' worth of hamburg and that was our main course. On Wednesday I bought ten cents' worth of sausage and Mrs. Stidger baked pancakes or buckwheat cakes. That was a meal then, fit for the gods, and still is in our family. On Thursday I went to the fish market downtown and bought a fresh salmon from the fishermen when they came in with their haul. That evening we had fresh salmon. On Friday evening we had salmon in a different way—only it was still salmon. On Saturday we had some of the salmon made into a nice salad and added to that the proverbial baked beans and brown bread—a Saturday evening eating habit we had picked up in New England and to which we still cling with joy. On Sunday, Mr. Mobbs, the grocer, always had us in for Sunday dinner, and what a dinner it was, enough to fill us up for two days. And we always carried home with us a big basketful of what was left over. It was mild survival of the old-time church donation custom of which Bishop Hughes speaks, and it was mighty welcome with us.

"How do they do it?" I have told of Bishop Hughes in his generation. Now I want to answer that quesiton through the expereince of a minister of this generation who is at this time the pastor of a church in a large manufacturing city on the Atlantic seaboard. I spoke in his church a short time ago. I knew that he had raised a family of four, had sent three of them to college, all of them graduating—one of them, a brilliant young girl, who earned a Ph.D. in addition to her regular academic degree and is now doing wonderful work in a specialized field. The youngest boy is just ready for college, for he will graduate from high school this spring.

I said to that man, "How did you do it, Jim?"

"Well, I have my top salary now, and it is only $2200. I pay my own rent. I keep up a small car—they expect me to have a car but they never expect to help in its upkeep or in my gas, oil, and tire bills. That is my lookout. I am expected to entertain every group of the church in my home and if I don't do it a question is raised as to my generosity. I am expected to dress neatly and to be an example of good grooming to young people. Right now we are planning to build a new church. We have raised close to seventy thousand dollars and have it in the bank, ninety per cent of which I raised myself. They all feel pretty smug and secure with that money gathering interest, waiting for times when we can build. They expect me to be a builder, a great executive, a great preacher, a great worker with young people, a financial wizard, and practically to build the church single-handed. They *must* expect me to be a financial wizard, for they have never raised my salary in five years in spite of the fact that I have raised their seventy thousand dollars. I still get what I received when I came to this church five years ago—just $2200—and pay my rent, and bills for upkeep of car, heat, and light. How do I dress my family and get them through college? I'll tell you: I do without things. I haven't had a new suit in five years. My wife hasn't had a new winter coat in more than that. When I talk about her getting a new coat she says: 'Mary is in college and she must look well. I can wait.' And she has waited—waited five years for that new coat, and it looks as if she will wait another two years, for our boy goes to college next fall. How do we do it? Well, for one thing, we do without a central heating system. We can't afford to rent a house with a central heating system in it, so I build and keep up fires in the old-fashioned way, in stoves and grates. I wish we had a central heating system, but we just cannot afford to have it. We try to keep up a scientific diet but we have no luxuries. If we have meat once a week we are happy. Chicken, turkey, ice cream—things we hear our parishioners talking about— well, they are just *out* for us. We don't even consider them.

"When I go down town to the preachers' meeting on Mondays most of the men stay for lunch and spend anywhere from fifty cents to a dollar for lunch. I wish I could stay with them and indulge in the luxury of eating with them; but it would deprive some one of my family of something he needs, and I just can't bring myself to doing it. I haven't eaten in a restaurant for five years, not since I came to this church. I can't afford it, but I have always taken out my tithe from the beginning.

"You ask me how we do it. Well, that is how we do it."

I came away from that visit and interview with little songs singing in my heart, a new sense of humility in my spirit, and a new sense of deep and profound admiration in my thoughts for that brave minister and his family.

"How DO they do it?" The answer is that there is always a spirit of co-operation in a ministerial household; they live meagrely, as has been illustrated in these stories of the boyhood home of Bishop Hughes and of a modern minister's home. However, the final answer to that question, "How DO they do it?" is the tithe and the spirit of stewardship. The minister teaches, preaches, and practices tithing, sharing, and stewardship, and that cannot be beaten for money-saving.

XXI

"GIVE IT TO JIMMIE!"

EDWIN MARKHAM, my poet friend of many years, caught
the spirit of giving in his most tender and beautiful Christmas poem, *The Manger Song of Mary*, the heart of which
is the spirit of giving which is always in the heart of a
mother and which was in the heart of Mary the Mother
of the Christ Child on that immemorable morning:

"Hark, baby, hark
    To the bells in the dark.
Here are the three that are led by the star—
Melchior, Gaspar and old Balthazar,
Great are the gifts in the hands of the wise—
Mother has only a kiss for your eyes!

"Croon, baby, croon
    Like a dove at the noon.
Melchior's beard, reaching down to the knees,
Pours you the gold from the hills and the seas,
Brings you a gift for a king to command—
Mother has only a kiss for your hand!

"Sleep, baby, sleep,
    For the shadows are deep.
Gaspar, with pearls on his red turban, comes,
Bringing you myrrh and Arabian gums.
Wind where he passes is warm, soft and sweet—
Mother has only a kiss for your feet!

"Dream, baby, dream,
    For the star is agleam,

Balthazar kneels by the manger to sing,
Burning white frankincense, ring over ring.
They have brought treasures from mountain and mart—
Mother has nothing to give but her heart!

In 1918 I was preaching in San Francisco. Every year of
my ministry I had made it a custom to visit some institution where I could watch the magnificent panorama of
Christmas in order to get the feel of Christmas those people experience who do not have homes in which to cele-
brate it. That year I visited the orphanage in Mill Valley.
There I learned, as many another minister has learned,
what Christmas really means.

I went early and spent the day in the orphanage. There
was a lot of excitement. But it was not all over the fact
that Christmas was the next day. It was mostly over the
fact that red-headed Jimmie was coming home from the
hospital. Jimmie was the favorite child at the orphanage.
He had tuberculosis of the skin. He had gone through
fifteen operations in two years. Everybody loved him, both
at the orphanage and at the hospital where he had spent
almost as much time as he had spent at the orphanage.

The matron could talk of nothing but the news that
Jimmie was coming home for Christmas. She showed me
the presents that had been sent in by friends. For weeks
bundles had been arriving daily. When they opened the
bundles and a particularly choice toy, cap, gun, or suit
showed up, some child would say, "Give it to Jimmie!
Give it to Jimmie!"

"That's the way we all feel about Jimmie," the matron
told me with tears in her motherly eyes.

"Even the collie dog loves him, because Jimmie is always doing something for him. He saves choice pieces of

meat and food and takes them out to feed the collie. The minute Jimmie goes into the yard that dog starts to romp, bark, and yip with joy."

As we walked through the rooms she added, "Jimmie has had all those awful operations, but how they love him down at the hospital. He said just before the last operation, 'Doc, I'll not cry; I'll stand anything if you'll only make me well. I've got so many things to do for the kids, the dog, and Mrs. Jones, and everybody. Just make me well and I don't care how much you hurt me!'

"The doctor says he wept that day and so did the nurse. They just couldn't help it. Jimmie was so brave and so kind, and always smiled—even when in intense pain after the operation. We all love him, and whenever there is something choice to eat they all yell 'Give it to Jimmie! Give it to Jimmie!' just as they do when a choice present comes in some bundle at the orphanage. 'Give it to Jimmie.'—that's almost our slogan."

"When is Jimmie coming home?" I asked, hoping that I might be there to see the homecoming.

"This afternoon at three o'clock," she replied, with a happy light in her eyes.

"I want to be here when he arrives."

Then it happened. I heard a commotion among the children; I heard a dog barking as if its joy knew no bounds. The matron also heard it, and we ran out into the yard. Sure enough, it was Jimmie coming home! The doctor loved him so much that he brought him home in his own car. He lifted Jimmie out. The crowd of children and nurses were all out in the yard to welcome the little fellow. The collie dog was beside himself, yelping, jumping, running about. It was a happy scene to watch. The

children laughed, yelled, wept, shouted. It was pande-
monium. Jimmie grinned and his red hair shone in the
California sun. They carried him into his room.

I came away from that experience confident that I had
discovered the real secret of Christmas. The secret was in
that phrase which all the children used when a choice
present was unearthed in a bundle and that wonderful
Christmas cry rang: "Give it to Jimmie! Give it to Jimmie!" And now that many years have passed, I have discovered no real reason to change my opinion about that.
The thing that makes a Christmas real is a "Give-it-to-Jimmie" attitude.

That Christmas stands out above all other Christmases
in my mind save one, and that too, strangely enough, was a
"Give it to Jimmie" Christmas.

It was in San Francisco and in my little church, called
Calvary, out in the sand dunes of the Sunset District,
where I had a poor family of eight children. It looked
as if they would not have much of a Christmas unless I
provided it for them, for the father had been out of work
for four months. One boy was a cripple; he had been left
deformed by infantile paralysis.

A week before Christmas I went to call on a new family
which had moved into the neighbourhood. They wanted
me to call for a special reason and had sent for me. I wondered what that particular reason for calling would turn
out to be. I went with eager curiosity.

I had hardly gotten seated when the mother, who had
asked me to call, began to tell me a strange story.

Her husband was an officer in the Navy. One winter,
when he was stationed in San Diego, California, and she
and little Billy, as she called her boy, were in New York

City visiting, an epidemic of diphtheria broke out and Billy died. She sold everything they owned but Billy's playthings, and left at once for San Diego to be with the father. Being a Navy family, they were moved about all over the world, but they always carried Billy's playthings with them; they could not bear to part with them. She kept them in a special trunk, and wherever they went she carried the little trunk along—to Manila, to South America one year; to Japan; another year to Siberia, and then a winter at the Panama Canal. It had been five years since Billy's death, and this year they were stationed in San Francisco.

All of this she told me as we sat in her home, and I was much impressed but still wondering why she had called me to tell me her story. Then her face brightened a bit and a tear rolled down her cheek.

"But I can't keep those playthings any longer, for last night I had a strange dream, Dr. Stidger. Billy came to me in the dream and told me that I must take all of those toys out of the trunk, and said, 'Mother, they do nobody any good in the trunk, and they make you feel sad every Christmas. I want you to take them out to some children who need them to have a merry Christmas.'"

Then in the dream, Billy told his mother what to do with every present in the trunk—the toy wagon, the drum, the bugle, the ship, the train, the clocks, the tank, and the policeman's hat. But it was the woolly dog that particularly interested him, for that had been his favorite toy, a little white woolly dog named Pershing. He wanted that to go to "a little crippled boy," he told his mother in the dream.

The mother turned to me and said, "I called you in to

ask if you happen to know of any family in your parish in which there is a little crippled boy who will not have any Christmas this year. For Billy's sake I want to make it a real Christmas for him.

It didn't take me long to tell her about the Browns, with their eight children, and little Billy, the cripple, for that, by a strange coincidence, was his name.

We spent the entire afternoon unpacking Billy's toys— toys that his mother had kept intact for five years, until she had that dream. Each year at Christmas she had unpacked the trunk, wept over the toys, and then carefully repacked them. So they were in good condition. There were enough for the entire Brown family.

Billy Brown had been in a plaster cast for years. The year before, at Christmas, he had had no presents at all. I happened to call on the family that year, and Billy said to me the day after Christmas, "I've been strapped in this old cast so long that when Christmas came I was just hoping for a surprise. I never wanted a surprise so much in all my life. I just knew that one would come. And sure enough one did come, for when I hung up my stocking and awoke in the morning there was nothing in it. I got my surprise all right! But I guess it isn't anybody's fault. Times are hard this year."

I could not tell, at first, whether the child's almost grown-up words and smile were the fruits of bitterness or sheer bravery. But I soon saw that his words were sheer bravery. Therefore, I determined that the next year he would get his surprise, if I could manage it.

And what a surprise that boy did have! The Navy officer's wife arranged that. She not only got out all of her own Billy's presents, but the two of us went shopping. We filled my old Ford with toys, oranges, candy, and food. There were dolls for the Brown girls, wagons, balls, bats, mechanical automobiles, and trains for the boys. It was the sort of Christmas that would delight the hearts of children who had never really known what a full, and generous Christmas could be. The Navy officer's wife went with me the night before Christmas, and, with the help of Mrs. Brown, we decorated a beautiful tree, and piled the gifts high on the floor. To little crippled Billy Brown went the woolly dog—just as the other Billy had requested in the dream. Christmas morning, as we walked to her home, the Navy officer's wife said to me: "This is the happiest Christmas I have had since Billy left me. I thought I could never bear to give away his toys, but he was right about that. You can't have Christmas happiness by keeping things—even memories. You have to pass them on to others."

I was so impressed with this experience and with the woman's reply as we walked home that the next year I told my young people in Calvary Church about it, and, spontaneously, a bright young girl said, "Well, let's organise a 'Give-it-to-Jimmie Club' in this church this Christmas, and hunt up some child or some family that will not have as bright a Christmas as we will, and see to it that they *do* have a good one."

I myself had not thought of that. I was just telling of my experience as a story to entertain them; but it caught on like wildfire, and that very evening we organised a "Give-it-to-Jimmie Christmas Club" and, so far as I know, that club is still going strong in that church.

That gave me an idea for every church I have served in the years since that far-away day in 1916. Every church which I have ministered to—in San Francisco, San José, California; Detroit, Michigan; Kansas City, Boston—all have organised "Give-it-to-Jimmie Christmas Clubs," and the idea has worked magnificently.

Some of the most beautiful and touching Christmas experiences I have known have come through this plan. In Calvary that first year our young people organised a "Give-it-to-Jimmie Club," and on Christmas Eve we visited Angel Island, where the Oriental immigrants come in. They presented a Christmas program, erected a brightly lighted Christmas tree, and gave presents to each Oriental who had landed that week. Three hundred were Chinese, who were being detained in quarantine. They had never heard the Christmas story. They were in a strange land, lonely, bewildered, baffled by this new experience. Our young people devoted an evening to them, with a lighted tree, oranges and candy, and some simple presents, a Bible, and a lot of beautiful Christmas spirit.

Then I told those Orientals the story of Christ. There was an interpreter to make them understand what Christmas meant, even if the gifts had not already done so. We closed by singing "Silent Night," and I tell you that those Orientals, usually of stolid face and unemotional eyes, had a strange, comprehending light in their faces.